How to Survive
The Internet

Paul R. Vlissidis

For more information, address: paul@vlissidis.com

FIRST EDITION

howtosurvivetheinternet.co.uk

For Jack, Clare, and Sophie

In memory of Sue

Acknowledgements

I owe a debt of thanks to my fellow *Hunted* Cyber Team members,
Doug Ipperciel, Richard Warren, Chris Mayhew, Derek Price,
and Sophia McCall; to my NCC Group colleagues; in particular
Nigel Gibbons, and to NCC Group itself for providing me with the
opportunities to work in cyber security over so many years.

I am most grateful to Linda Fernley for her editing.

I would like to thank Claudia Joseph, whose article got me introduced
to the *Hunted* production team.

Finally, I must single out a particular friend and colleague for
special thanks; Lloyd Brough first suggested that I should write a
book about this subject and he has been a sounding board for my
ideas throughout.

Illustrations by Felix Yarwood

Cover design by Jason Anscomb

Table of Contents

Chapter 1: Introduction..1

Chapter 2: How did we get here?...17

Chapter 3: Determine your digital footprint 33

Chapter 4: Reduce your digital footprint......................................57

Chapter 5: Protect your accounts – The Password Problem............91

Chapter 6: Protect your privacy online 109

Chapter 7: Secure your home against cyber attack...................... 129

Chapter 8: Travel and mobile device security 155

Chapter 9: How to deal with an attack 183

Chapter 10: What does the future hold? 203

Chapter 1: Introduction

I have been immersed in cyber security since before it was even called cyber security. I led the cyber team on seasons one to five of the popular UK Channel 4 TV show, *Hunted*,[1] and seasons one, two and three of *Celebrity Hunted*,[2] where we effectively used the same techniques as hackers, cyber criminals, and cyber stalkers to track the fugitives and their close associates for 28 days. Of course, we had permission for everything we did and informed consent, but while shooting the first celebrity series of *Hunted* I began to realise that our digital lives had reached a tipping point where the complexity of the technology and our knowledge of how to use it securely had diverged significantly. Bluntly, most people don't know how to use technology securely and this contributes to the stress of modern life. People worry that their data isn't secure but don't feel empowered to do anything about it. I decided to gather together into a single place as much information and guidance as I felt people needed to be able to confidently use this amazing technology that has transformed our lives.

This book is designed to help ordinary, everyday users of the Internet to improve their resilience against hackers and cyber attacks and allow them to lead their online lives in 'quiet enjoyment', to use a legal term. Nothing can protect you totally from attack – not even removing yourself from the Internet, as your data will still be stored by companies you interact with – but you should be aware of those

---

[1]   http://www.channel4.com/programmes/hunted

[2]   https://www.channel4.com/programmes/celebrity-hunted

aspects of your online life you can control, those you can't, and what you can do about it. This book will help you understand how you are exposed and what steps to take to protect yourself and your loved ones from the hackers, the stalkers – and the advertisers. My aim throughout is to demystify Internet security and bring a modicum of assurance to everyone's lives.

Increasing numbers of people are so worried about privacy and security online that they're leaving many of the platforms. I don't think that self-isolating is the right way to behave as it's not addressing the issue but rather, trying to duck it. Our online lives are only going to get richer and more complicated, so I want us to embrace the technology in a way that doesn't leave us exposed to hackers and advertisers. In a National Cyber Security Centre (NCSC) 2019 survey,[3] only 15% of respondents said they knew a great deal about how to protect themselves online.

If you've ever had your pocket picked, you'll know that feeling when you suddenly discover your wallet is missing or your phone is gone, or both. There is a moment of confusion when you tell yourself that you must have left it in the car, or the café you just visited. Perhaps you've forgotten to bring it with you and then you recall that you had it a few minutes ago and now it's gone. It's a particularly unpleasant feeling and, even though no violence has taken place, you still feel violated. As well as the financial impact, there is a significant emotional impact; you're left with a sense of shame that you were so gullible.

---

[3] https://www.ncsc.gov.uk/news/most-hacked-passwords-revealed-as-uk-cyber-survey-exposes-gaps-in-online-security

Discovering you're a victim of cybercrime is similar, but cybercrime is even more surreptitious. In most cases you don't even find out you're a victim until sometime after the event, and when you do find out it's often in the most unpleasant manner – some money has been transferred or some pictures have been posted. There is the same confusion: "surely I haven't been hacked? There must be some mistake?" Then the realisation dawns on you. What's different about cybercrime is that you often don't know how or when the attack happened. Nor do you know how deeply the attackers have infiltrated your online life. That 'pit of the stomach' feeling lasts a lot longer than having your pocket picked. What can you do to get your money back? What can you do to prevent it from happening again? Many victims of cybercrime suffer significant levels of trauma. In most cases, there is a financial loss to the victim – a loss that gets greater when stolen data is sold on and reused by other criminals. Victims often feel that there has been an invasion of their privacy. After hackers leaked naked photos of Jennifer Lawrence in 2014, the actress said it was a "sexual violation". It's the very same feelings that victims of assault experience. They're upset, they're depressed, they feel guilt. From a behavioural standpoint, victims can suffer insomnia and eating disorders, needing time off work to sort everything out. In the more extreme cases, the victims have been so traumatised by the possibility of the data becoming public that they take their own lives, as happened in the Ashley Madison[4] breach, when two people committed suicide after email threats to expose them.[5] The financial impact can be extreme, extending well beyond a few credit card transactions. In 2017, a couple had their email hacked during

---

[4]   https://en.wikipedia.org/wiki/Ashley_Madison_data_breach

[5]   https://www.bbc.co.uk/news/technology-34044506

the sale of a flat and were scammed out of over £300,000[6] when the scammers posed as the couple and sent emails to their solicitor with fraudulent bank details.

The emotional impact to the victim is more long-lasting in instances when data is actually used and abused. If you have never been a victim, it can be difficult to understand the trauma. The following 'tableaux' are fictionalised accounts of victims of cybercrime. The stories are made up from a concoction of actual incidents and outcomes that have been reported to me by victims at talks and conferences where I've spoken.

---

[6] https://www.thisismoney.co.uk/money/mortgageshome/article-4248340/My-estate-agent-sent-deposit-flat-Mr-Jihad.html

Meet Amelia

Amelia is a 27-year-old marketing executive in London. She lives with four flatmates and commutes to work every day on the bus. Amelia is a millennial, so a full 'digital native', and embraces all things new. She has carried a phone and a laptop since she was 12 and experiences real anxiety if parted from either.

Amelia has a rich digital life, with accounts on all the main social media platforms, and regularly posts stories on Snapchat and Instagram. She found her flat online, her job online, and buys most of her clothes online. She has recently bought a smart bulb for her room and a digital home assistant for her music. She also writes a 'tell-all' Twitter blog about the world of marketing under a pseudonym.

Amelia has recently finished a relationship with Joe. They were together for two years, but Amelia ended it after the arguments had become what seemed to define their relationship.

On the bus one Monday morning, Amelia sees a new direct message from Duncan, someone she met at the weekend, flash up on her lock screen. She thinks it will be seen as too keen to read it straight away, so she doesn't open the app. At lunchtime she decides to check the message but when she looks it has gone. At first Amelia thinks she must have got the wrong app but when she opens her other messaging apps, they are all devoid of messages from Duncan. Did she dream it? That evening she gets home and prepares to publish a story on Instagram. As she's adding photos from her library, she realises that some photos from the weekend are missing – particularly the party on Saturday. Now she's starting to get concerned.

What's going on?

As Amelia is going to bed, she sees that she has several Facebook messages. To her horror she sees several people from work have accepted friend requests from her. She knows she didn't friend them; in fact, she can't stand several of them and has posted about them to close friends. Nervously she goes back through her timeline and, to her horror, sees that several of those conversations have now been shared with her new 'friends'. How will she face them in the office tomorrow? When she wakes up, she sees a message from the anonymous Twitter account that she uses to blog about the world of marketing. The message says her account has been suspended due to racist remarks. Racist remarks? Amelia opens the app and sees that 'she' has tweeted a vile image with an extreme hate speech caption. What's worse, the tweet is followed by another containing a picture of Amelia along with her name, address, and mobile phone number, stating she is the owner of the account.

How did this happen? Amelia's ex-partner Joe knew Amelia's passwords and she hadn't changed them since they split. He regularly stalked her social media accounts and when he saw the message from Duncan, became jealous and started a campaign of malicious posting using her accounts.

Meet Greg

Greg is a 35-year-old credit controller in Manchester. He is not a major user of online services such as social media but does like to shop for cycling gear online to feed his passion for all things bike. He tends to use his phone and tablet for everything online and doesn't own a laptop. Greg is engaged and about to buy a new flat and move in with his fiancée.

One weekend Greg gets an email from one of his online shopping accounts saying there been a data breach and he is a victim. He is assured that no credit card details were taken but as a matter of precaution he will be getting contacted by his bank regarding a replacement card. Greg is mildly annoyed but changes his password as the shop instructs him to do and thinks nothing more about it as his mind is busy with sorting out a mortgage for his new flat, where their offer has just been accepted. He is getting to the deposit stage and a few days later he emails the conveyancer to ask where he should transfer the money. He receives an email within an hour giving him the bank details and proceeds to make the transfer. The following day Greg gets a call asking when he will make the transfer. Greg explains that he has already done so but the conveyancer says no money has arrived. Greg rechecks his emails and notices that there are two emails with bank details, one of which (the real one) is in his deleted items.

How did this happen? Greg also used his shopping site password for his email, and the hackers with access to his shopping site username and password used a tool to automatically check the stolen credentials on other online services. Having gained access to his email they saw his conveyancing request and quickly spoofed a reply with fake bank details after deleting the real one.

As I mentioned, these scenarios are fictional, although based on reported events. This last example, however, is completely factual. A few years ago, I was fortunate enough to have the opportunity to work with a journalist to find out what it's like to have your life invaded by hackers. Claudia Joseph (author and journalist) contacted me to ask for help with a follow-up to a story she had written several years before. The original story had been about data protection, and had showed that a Data Subject Access request under the 1998 UK Data Protection Act could provide a stranger with enough information to steal someone's identity. Now, Claudia wanted to see if anything had changed and to update her readers on the new dangers of identity theft online. What would happen if somebody was able to infiltrate your online life? Claudia contacted me in late 2013 and started the conversation with "Can you hack me?" I had to explain that we would need all sorts of permissions in place before we could do something like this. Indeed, we would have to almost devise a power of attorney to allow me to access her online life.

Working in cyber security, exploring the security of technology is nothing new to me. My team's background was in finding and fixing vulnerabilities in companies' computer systems and networks to protect them from hackers – sometimes called ethical hacking – but this was different. I would be digging deeper into the life of an individual, operating as a real-life hacker, and actively looking to exploit the weak links. This was to be a disturbing experience for both sides, and a reality check that I was not prepared for.

With all legal permissions in place and with a couple of caveats – no irreparable damage, no changing passwords on certain accounts – I began work on the project. My initial research was more challenging than I'd anticipated – her Facebook account was locked down, and her Twitter account was only used to link to articles she had written. I wasn't getting close to obtaining the credentials I would need to get into her life. Claudia had also been sly, in that all communications to us until then had been via a 'burner'[7] Hotmail account. We targeted this immediately and were able to reset her password (with permission) but it led nowhere (an old iTunes account that showed she had bought music back in 2006). This suggested she was an Apple user. Then, at last, a breakthrough.

Through her email address and a read receipt from her phone, I was able to confirm she was a current Apple user. Several possibilities presented themselves. We crafted and tested a working attack on her Safari browser, so we just needed her to click a link in a phishing email but, as luck would have it, Apple released a set of patches the weekend before we planned to use it. Claudia had already told me she kept up to date with patches, so my spirits dropped. My colleagues and I went back to the drawing board. We knew Claudia was alert to phishing attacks under normal circumstances – even more so, as she was aware that we were trying to hack her – but nevertheless we thought we could use her Apple account as bait. I had told her when we initially spoke that we might try phishing, but I also told her that we might cause some of her accounts to become blocked. We therefore used a phishing attack based on unblocking her Apple id. This worked and opened a goldmine – access to her iCloud account.[8]

---

[7]   An account usually used for only one purpose and then discarded

[8]   The method we used at the time would not work today, as security measures have improved

The security of the cloud isn't something that is only of concern to Apple users. Google, Android, Microsoft, and others all have information that hackers would love to get their hands on. Using a single username and password with (at that time) no additional security measures meant I was able to gain access to all Claudia's emails, all her contact information (including her bank details, which were stored in her contact list), and discover her whereabouts at any time using 'Find My iPhone'. I was even able to clone her phone,[9] which was backed up to iCloud, and provided access to all her photos and apps as well as her passwords. Her photo stream appeared on our clone in real time and, using the geotags, we could see where she was standing. I sent her back some google earth images of where she was at the time, which freaked her out.

Welcome emails from shops, energy companies, and travel providers helped me to identify her accounts and even transfer money. I could get into her mobile account and send text messages purporting to be from her; I could see all her travel patterns on her travel card so could work out where she was likely to be at any given time on any day of the week. Bear in mind I was just using credentials to access these accounts.

I was set various challenges, all of which I was able to achieve. I found out who her neighbours were and which of them were her friends, and I found out what car she drove using a car selling website and typing in her registration number. I sent a text as Claudia asking a neighbour to let me into her house while she was away (Claudia confirmed the neighbour waited in for me to carry out

---

[9] This would be much harder with modern iCloud accounts

her instructions). I saw her photos, I knew what books she read, what beauty products she used – and by accessing her social media accounts, I could see that I would have been able to get into the lives of many of her friends. Claudia asked me to identify who she was staying with in India, and through email and direct message conversations this was easy. I also noted that the husband of her host (an old school friend) worked at a foreign Embassy. It's interesting to note that a trust relationship with my target now potentially exposed her friends, though of course we never crossed the permission line.

This is more disturbing than someone who simply wants to steal your credit card details, which, perhaps ironically, we never actually got. This is, of course, a traumatic experience in the same way that a burglary leaves you feeling violated and vulnerable. But a malicious ex-partner, for example, could do a great deal more damage on an emotional level. Many people share their security information with people they love, but if the relationship breaks down, do you change your passwords as well as your locks? The whole experiment was a shock to the system for both of us, making me appreciate just how prurient and unpleasant it would be to have somebody in your life to such an extent. I felt genuinely uncomfortable with the level of access to Claudia's life that I now had.

One of the most worrying aspects of the whole experiment was that I believe Claudia was then (and certainly is now) probably a great deal more security-savvy than the vast majority of people, and this has been confirmed by my subsequent experience on *Hunted*. To me, that suggests that we in the security industry have failed. We expect too much from our users by believing they have enough skill and knowledge to use our technologies securely, rather than giving them security 'out of the box☐. As systems become more complex, and increasingly more of our life is lived online, we also become more vulnerable. Security professionals seem to delight in confusing non-security people by using jargon, and we quite like the slightly scary image that our role lends us, thanks largely to TV and movies.

Following the experiment, Claudia has now implemented multi-layered security for her online life and made use of technologies, like password managers, to help ensure she has unique, complex passwords for each website. The providers have also moved on, and much of what we did back then would not work now, but hackers' techniques have also evolved, and these types of attacks are still happening. The story appeared in the *Mail on Sunday* and you can read it at

https://www.dailymail.co.uk/news/article-2527677/How-life-stolen-cyber-stalkers-They-took-cash-job-keys-home-simply-hacking-emails-And-Christmas-planning-you.html

So, what about you? Perhaps you haven't changed your password in a while? That's no big deal, right? It's a fairly complex password, so nobody is going to crack it. Okay, Okay, you know you should be using

a password manager and regularly updating your phone, but it is so much easier just having the one password and ignoring the prompts from your phone vendor. Most hacks aren't from state actors, but are likely to be from colleagues, friends, partners (current or ex), or opportunist criminals. I will outline why these attacks succeed and how you can take steps so that you are not an easy victim.

The emphasis throughout the book is on practical and accessible advice. Web links occur throughout the book and I have placed these either in the body of the text or in footnotes. I have attempted to provide links or search terms that will get you directly to the detailed step-by-step advice, although the sands of the web shift quickly, and can easily bury web pages, so you may get some '404' errors. You can find all of the links on the book's companion website:

https://howtosurvivetheinternet.co.uk	

If one link fails, I suggest you use a search engine with the referring sentence, and you should get the updated link. Where URLs are longer, I have used QR codes to make it easier. Most modern phones can read them directly. In some cases, you will need to login to get to the page. If you are unfamiliar with QR codes you can find a useful guide at https://www.lifewire.com/scan-qr-codes-on-smartphone-4154658

I'm keenly aware that different readers have different risk appetites and comfort levels with using technology, and privacy means different things to different people. Almost everyone needs a basic level of security, and most want to avoid embarrassment or personal loss though inadvertent privacy problems. Therefore, as well as covering all the 'basics', I will also include advice for the more privacy minded who really want to lock things down tight and keep them that way. I hope this will be a 'one-stop' shop for you for all things associated with personal cyber security.

I will use 'chilli scores' on all my suggestions as follows:

Difficulty rating	Description
	Essential privacy setting – protects you from being an easy victim. Easy to do.
	Extra peace of mind – you will be much harder to attack and any attack on one of your service providers will be contained. May require a little effort or a change in behaviour.
	Very privacy minded setting or activity for the more technically adventurous/ skilled. Will definitely involve some effort, time, and perhaps some research.

To participate in a digital life, there are some risks we just have to accept. We can't prevent hackers from getting access to things we don't control, but we can improve our resilience by making sure that the digital footprint we leave is small(er), the data that matters to us is preserved, and the accounts that hold our most important and personal information are protected and monitored. This will be our quest.

Chapter 2: How did we get here?

"The Russians are coming!"

"The Chinese are already here!"

"North Korea carries out massive
WannaCry cyber-attack!"

"The world could stop as a result of cyber attacks!"

These are typical of the headlines about cyber security these days but for most of us this is far removed from our daily online experience and, for most of us, being hacked is a relatively rare occurrence. That said, given the amount of time we spend online it's not surprising that each of us at some point during our online lifetime will be the victim of a hack. Sometimes this is entirely unwitting and results from a company, that we have trusted with our personal details, being hacked and our details traded on the Dark Web. The first we get to hear about it is a letter telling us our details have been compromised. There is a widely held belief that there is nothing we can do about this – that it's entirely out of our control. But that's not true; there is much we can do to protect ourselves online such that the impact of these types of attack is reduced to nothing at all or, in many cases, a relatively minor nuisance instead of a major event such as identity theft, which can be extraordinarily difficult to recover from.

To help us understand why some of the measures I'm proposing are necessary, I think it's worth asking how we got where we are today.

A brief history of hacking

Hacking became 65 years old in 2020 – old enough to draw a pension! It may be an activity often associated in the media with young people but hacking itself is middle-aged. Hacking didn't begin as a term describing criminal activity; in fact it was a term first used in 1955 at the Massachusetts Institute of Technology (MIT) to describe people who liked to tinker with technology, and has retained this meaning (as well as the negative one) ever since. The first nefarious hacking activity is attributed to people getting free phone calls by whistling down the telephone (using a toy flute) starting around 1957. That was called 'phreaking' but it planted the seeds of what was to become the hacking subculture.

PHONE PHREAKING

Phone phreaks spent a lot of time exploring the telephone network to understand how systems worked. They listened to the clicks and whistles to determine how calls were routed. They acquired telephone company technical manuals. They impersonated operators and other telephone company personnel (what we now call social engineering). They even broke into telephone company buildings at night and wired up their own telephones. They built devices called blue boxes, black boxes, and red boxes to help them make free phone calls. They wrote their own newsletters to spread information.

The first issue of the hacker magazine *Phrack* was in November 1985.

The first widely accepted reference to malicious hacking is 'telephone hackers' in MIT's student newspaper, *The Tech*, which described in 1963 how hackers tied up the lines at Harvard by configuring the PDP-1 computer to make free calls, so-called 'war dialling' (see panel later in this chapter), and accumulating large phone bills.

Vol. 83, No. 24 Cambridge, Mass., Wednesday, Nov. 20, 1963 5c

Services curtailed

Telephone hackers active

By Henry Lichstein

Many telephone services have been curtailed because of so-called hackers, according to Professor Carlton Tucker, administrator of the Institute phone system.

Stating "It means the students who are doing this are depriving the rest of you of privileges you otherwise might have," Prof. Tucker noted that two or three students are expelled each year for abuses on the phone system.

The hackers have accomplished such things as tying up all the tie-lines between Harvard and MIT, or making long-distance calls by charging them to a local radar installation. One method involved connecting the PDP-1 computer to the phone system to search the lines until a dial tone, indicating an outside line, was found.

Tie lines connect MIT's phone

Next The Tech

system to many areas without a prorata charge. Among the tie-lines discovered have been ones to the Millstone Radar Facility, the Sudbury defense installation, IBM in Kingston, New York, and the MITRE Corporation.

Tucker warns hackers

Commenting on these incidents, Prof. Tucker said "If any of these people are caught (by the telephone company) they are liable to be put in jail. I try to warn them and protect them."

While Tucker felt " we don't have too much trouble with the boys; we appreciate their curiosity," he also said that repeated involvement, for instance, caused the expulsion from the Institute of one member of the Class of '63 one week before his graduation.

Because of the "hacking", the majority of the MIT phones are "trapped". They are set up so tie-line calls may not be made. Originally, these tie-lines were open to general use.

Lines Found by Force

While the hackers have resorted to some esoteric methods, many tielines have been found by "brute force techniques" — mass dialing until something "interesting" is found. Another, more urbane method, has been the judicious perusal of telephone directories. To quote one accomplished hacker, "The field is always open to experimentation."

While stating "We attempt to stop (hacking) because it impairs our relations with the phone company, and hurts the service for the rest of the students," Tucker observed that the MIT phone system, serving a community of about 14,000 persons, is as large as that for a small town.

Including Lincoln Laboratories, which accounts for over 50% of costs, the Institute's phone bill exceeds $1,000,000 each year. This is the third largest bill in New England.

The General Electric Company has the largest phone bill. Raytheon Corporation has the second largest bill in the New England area.

In 1971, one 'phreak', John Draper (who became known by the hacker handle "Cap'n Crunch"), discovered that a toy whistle given away inside Cap'n Crunch cereal generated a 2,600-hertz signal, the same high-pitched tone needed to access AT&T's long-distance switching system when issued down the phone mouthpiece. Ron Rosenbaum wrote "Secrets of the Little Blue Box" in *Esquire* magazine, with instructions for making a blue box – a device to use combinations of tones to manipulate (i.e. hack) the telephone system. Among the readers were two college kids, Steve Wozniak and Steve Jobs, future founders of Apple Computer, who launched a home industry making and selling blue boxes.

The start of modern hacking subculture is often attributed to a short essay entitled "The Conscience of a Hacker" (also known as "The Hacker Manifesto"), which was published in the first issue of the hacker magazine *Phrack* in January 1986.[10] It has stood the test of time remarkably well. It addresses themes such as the feeling of intellectual alienation, frustration at the education system, and the idea that there is a community of like-minded individuals whose main 'crime' is that of curiosity. It does not consider victims because at that time the victims of hacking were mostly phone companies, academic institutions, and governments.

---

[10] http://phrack.org/issues/7/3.html

WAR DIALING

War dialing was the activity of systematically dialing hundreds or thousands of telephone numbers to identify computers connected to the network via devices called 'modems'.

In the early days of the Internet, computers would communicate using the public telephone network by literally dialing other computers using a device called a modem. Almost all computer networks used modems and devices called acoustic couplers to send data via tones over normal phone lines at that time. Calling these numbers could get you a login prompt, from which the hack could begin.

War dialing was a way of 'scanning' for computers by dialing numbers looking for modem signals, as a precursor to hacking them.

Famously, war dialing is used in the movie *War Games* starring Matthew Broderick – a 'must see' for anyone interested in the history of hacking.

For many years, hacking was confined to these enthusiasts and politically inspired groups (sometimes called 'hacktivists'), with little or no impact on you and I. But in 1986 a systems administrator at the Lawrence Berkeley National Laboratory, Clifford Stoll, noted certain small irregularities in accounting data. Pioneering the first digital forensic techniques, he determined that an unauthorised user was hacking into his computer network. Documented in his seminal (and highly recommended) book *The Cuckoo's Egg*,[11] Stoll used what we now call a 'honey pot' to lure a hacker into the network until enough evidence could be gathered to identify the perpetrator. Stoll's efforts and tenacity resulted in the arrest of Markus Hess and a number of others located in West Germany, who were stealing and selling military information, passwords, and other data to the KGB.

So, perhaps unsurprisingly, the new Internet was being exploited by spies to access secrets decades ago.

In 1988, Robert Morris, a student at Cornell University, created what would be known as the first 'worm'[12] on the Internet – just to give himself an idea of the size of the global network. The worm was released from a computer at MIT in 1988 (perhaps the first example of Internet malware misattribution). It began as a supposedly harmless prank but quickly became a devastating denial of service attack, as a bug in the worm's propagation algorithm led to computers being infected at a rate much faster than Morris had anticipated. It turns out that hackers are often not particularly good programmers, and that remains true to this day. This pre-dated any sort of Antivirus software so computers were utterly defenceless. By the time he realised the issue and attempted to rectify it by telling systems operators how to kill the worm, many systems had been affected. Morris became the first person to be convicted of violating the US Computer Fraud and Abuse Act, and malware had arrived.

---

[11] https://en.wikipedia.org/wiki/The_Cuckoo%27s_Egg
[12] A worm is a self-replicating computer program

The fascination of getting machines to behave in ways the designers never intended has remained compelling to the tech community. Couple this with the universal attraction of an anarchic activity that is breaking the rules (or the law), and you have a heady mix that continues to attract the technically curious to both the 'dark side' and the security industry.

In 1990, Tim Berners-Lee completed his build out of all the components necessary for his 'World Wide Web' project – a web server, a web browser, a web editor, and the first web pages. In 1991, he made his project publicly available on the Internet as the 'Web'. Between 1990 and 1999, the Web grew to over 17 million websites – today it is over 1.5 billion. This was a low-risk, high-return environment for the community of hackers. In a Darwinian ecosystem such niches get exploited fast, and this was no exception. The hacktivists and cyber criminals started to move in and exploit all the easy pickings offered by these websites.

The cost of getting online was around $2.95 per hour (plus the cost of the call) in 1995. In today's money that would be over $2,000 per month for a modern typical Internet user. This cost fell dramatically with the widespread introduction of broadband Internet in the early 2000s.

By the mid-2000s, the perfect conditions for cybercrime had formed: there was a huge increase in the number of Internet users, with lots of people conducting online banking and purchases; there were very few resources to investigate and prosecute cybercrime; weak legislation, and almost no regulation; and widespread poor security.

With the introduction of mobile Internet and the advent of devices such as the Apple iPhone, the number of users grew at an almost exponential rate. As each naïve user joined the exciting new environment, the average level of Internet security awareness fell slightly – something that remains true today – and the conditions for criminals became easier by the day.

In all those years, it was always companies that were the main target of the phreak and the hacker. In the early days it was telecoms companies who were attacked to provide free access, but as the Internet grew and developed, other companies soon became targets. In the intervening 30-odd years little has changed in this regard except that there are many more hackers than in the 1980s, the tools and techniques have become widespread, and in recent years the space once occupied by curious geeks has now been claimed by organised criminal gangs. Company networks remain the hackers' targets of choice but the data they are after is almost always about you, the citizen.

The widespread sharing culture in the hacking community caused a trickle-down effect, whereby malware and hacking techniques were rapidly copied – often by less technically proficient hackers (called 'script kiddies'). This had the effect of spreading the problem far and wide, and at great speed.

Before we all went online ourselves, the data about us was largely confined to financial information held by banks and there was no significant black market – although stolen credit cards have been traded (known as 'carding') since the mid-1990s. Now the variety and volume of information held about us has burgeoned to the point where crimes like identity theft are frighteningly easy to perpetrate. As well as the organised criminal gangs (OCGs), we still have politically-motivated hackers (hacktivists), who have been joined by state-sponsored hackers and, more recently, cyber stalkers who have personal motives against individuals.

Stalking and harassment have always existed, but since the growth of the Internet, it has become easier for those who carry it out to do so either as an extension of their existing activities, or purely online. Cyber stalking goes beyond nuisance and can cause severe distress and mental trauma.

According to the National Centre for Cyberstalking Research,[13] over 90% of us have experienced some form of harassment online. Of these cases, 21% were linked to total strangers, but 61% were known to the victim. A particularly harrowing account appeared in *Wired* magazine in 2016.[14] In November 2012, stalking became a named offence in England and Wales for the first time.

Hacking has been illegal for much longer and yet remains a low-risk, high-reward activity. Despite significant efforts to regulate, legislate, and monitor Internet activity, the overwhelming majority of hacking goes undetected and unpunished. There are plenty of statistics to back me up here, but the one that stands out for me is the number of publicly known (that is to say, accessible if you know where to look)

---

[13] https://www.beds.ac.uk/irac/about/centres/nccr/publications/
https://www.beds.ac.uk/irac/about/centres/nccr/echo/

[14] https://www.wired.com/2016/02/
ive-had-a-cyberstalker-since-i-was-12/

'breached' website accounts. The current statistic can be found on Troy Hunt's website, haveibeenpwned.com, but at the time of writing the figure is north of 10 billion accounts. When you consider this doesn't include some of the largest breaches reported (Yahoo, for example), the figure is staggering.

For many people, the criminal threat actors aren't the main worry; for them, it's the Internet Service Providers and the platforms themselves, and their reputed tendency to ride roughshod over our privacy, that bothers them the most.

The Internet has sometimes been referred to as the Wild West. This is not entirely fair, but it does contain a central truth. The Wild West was a land of opportunity but full of dangers and largely unregulated. Any citizen venturing west of the Mississippi River was advised to do so only if they were properly defended. I think that this analogy stands up in the current climate. Efforts to regulate the Internet have been few and far between, and some would say this is a good thing as it provides the best environment for innovation and freedom. I'm not advocating heavy regulation – I'm a realist in this regard. Instead, I would suggest that all of us who want to live part or most of our lives in cyberspace should do so only if we have some decent defences.

Can you have a large digital footprint and maintain a reasonable level of cyber resilience? Yes, you can, and this book will show you how. But as Kevin Mitnick (at one time the world's most wanted hacker) says: "You can never protect yourself 100%. What you do is protect yourself as much as possible and mitigate risk to an acceptable degree. You can never remove all risk."

You may feel that it's not unreasonable to expect your Internet Service Provider (ISP) to protect you, but most of the risks are entirely out of their control. It would be like expecting the roadbuilders or local authorities who manage them to protect all drivers from accidents. There are certainly things that providers could do but thus far security has not become a differentiator in decisions to buy or consume Internet services. I think that is changing, but slowly. Legislators are reluctant to act, as most of the measures they could come up with would appear draconian and be limited by jurisdiction, whereas the Internet is (essentially) a jurisdiction-free environment. Had today's problems been foreseen by the founders, it may have been significantly different. One of those founders, Sir Tim Berners-Lee, said: "We demonstrated that the Web had failed instead of served humanity, as it was supposed to have done, and failed in many places." The increasing centralisation of the Web, he says, has "ended up producing – with no deliberate action of the people who designed the platform – a large-scale emergent phenomenon which is anti-human".

Anatomy of an attack

So how do you get attacked? For most of us a targeted attack seems unlikely, so how do we become victims of hackers? What is the process that hackers go through to get your credentials or send you malware?

The first thing to understand is that every time you give up your email address, mobile phone number, or enter a password you are entrusting that information to a third party who may sell it, lose it by being hacked, or abuse it directly.

Email is the most common piece of information that we give away. Even if we leave a false name on a website and a dodgy address, we probably use a valid email address. I strongly advise everyone to have at least two email addresses – a 'proper' one for all your daily activities and a 'throwaway' one for all those website registrations you have to go through just to get the voucher or the download. You can then register both emails with a website called https:// haveibeenpwned.com . If either of these emails appears in a public data breach, you will get informed. More on this later.

The problem with email is that, as well as a means to communicate with you, it's almost always used as the username on websites. So just possession of your email address automatically gives hackers the first 50% of what they need to log in to all the online accounts associated with that email.

WHY THE NAME 'SPAM'?

The name comes from spam luncheon meat by way of a *Monty Python* sketch in which spam is ubiquitous, unavoidable, and repetitive.

Email spam has steadily grown since the early 1990s, and by 2014 was estimated to make up around 90% of email messages sent.

Most webmail systems do a good job of filtering out spam, so its nuisance value has fallen over time.

Spam 'bots' are autonomous software programs designed to collect, or harvest, email addresses from the Internet in order to build mailing lists for sending unsolicited email.

Somehow, despite all the privacy promises made by all the websites you sign up for, that email address finds its way into a spam list and before long you start getting all those emails from people you never heard of in your junk folder. It's just part of your online life so you accept it, but it's also important to understand that the email address is now 'out there'. To give a sense of the enormous scale of this, let's look at some of these spam lists.

In 2017, a spam 'bot' called Onliner was discovered with a list of 711 million email addresses. The emails it sent out had a 'phone home' web GIF image – just one pixel in size – which meant that when the email was opened, the link was activated and the spam server could validate that the email address was 'live'. This is why you shouldn't open spam email at all, and especially **don't unsubscribe**. Clicking "Unsubscribe" in a scammer's email will not usually result in your email address being removed from the scammer's email list. What it will do is verify to the scammer that your email address is in fact a valid and active address (which will have the unwanted side effect of making your email address even more valuable to the scammer in the future). Clicking unsubscribe may also take you to a malicious website that will download malware onto your computer and/or trick you into falling for a scam offer of some sort. You didn't "subscribe" to all those junk emails in the first place, so trying to "unsubscribe" from them is a waste of your time. It's actually worse than a waste of time – it's dangerous! Just leave them untouched in your junk folder.

How data breaches are used by cybercriminals

So, your email address is out there. The problem is that some of the legitimate websites you have signed up for have been victims of hacking, and their user databases have been stolen. Nowadays, with the arrival of privacy legislation such as the EU's General Data Protection Regulation (GDPR), you should get informed if this data is stolen or compromised (assuming the data owner knows about it), but until 2018 there was no obligation on the website owner to inform you of these data breaches. Consequently, your username (email) and password for that website are out there. Once the original hacker who obtained the database has finished with it or sold it, it will eventually appear somewhere on the so-called 'Dark Web' for use by everyone. This is another source of spam lists – compromised email addresses, but, even worse, these emails come with passwords. These 'data breaches' or 'password dumps' have been a game changer for hackers. The availability of billions (yes, billions) of user account details has spawned a hacking industry. I will discuss data breaches and how to defend yourself in Chapter 5. Many of these data breaches get combined into vast lists and have names such as Collection #1 and AntiPublic; AntiPublic has over 500 million account details.

How 'credential stuffing' works

The practice of taking these data breaches and trying out all the usernames and password on multiple websites is called credential stuffing. It relies on the fact that many (all?) of us reuse passwords between websites. Here's how it works. This is a real story, but I've changed the names of the victims.

In early 2019, criminal hackers used the AntiPublic data breach to log onto the little-used Facebook account of, let's call him Pete. Pete had no idea that his credentials were in a data breach and even if he got the email, he didn't think to change that password on his other accounts.

Having accessed his Facebook account, the hackers then contacted 50 of Pete's friends using messenger. Let's pick one of those friends; we'll call him Steve. The messenger conversation went something like this:

Pete: "Hi, How's it going Steve?"

Steve: "Good thanks, how are you?"

Pete: "I'm good but was wondering if you could do me a favour? I'm clearing out my garage and selling some old laptops on eBay, but I don't have a PayPal account. Would it be ok to have the buyer deposit the money into your PayPal and you send it to me later?"

Steve: "I wouldn't want to give you my bank details."

Pete: "No, that's fine just your email is all I need."

Steve: "Ok, the email for my PayPal is <email address>"

Pete: "Great thanks! I really appreciate this. There are a few laptops so expect a few deposits over the next few days."

Steve: "Ok no problem."

Pete: "Almost forgot – I will let you know once all the sales are complete and could you then just transfer the money to me at <uk sort code and account number>?"

Steve: "Sure, will do."

Over the next couple of days there were nine deposits of around £500 each, totalling £4,500. Steve duly transferred the money from his PayPal to the bank account 'Pete' had given him. All seemed fine; after all, Steve had just passed on money that wasn't his. Then Steve got a message from PayPal saying that refunds had been issued on all nine transactions and the money had been debited from his PayPal balance. Steve now owed PayPal £4,500. Of course, Steve contacted the real Pete and asked what was going on. Pete, of course, knew nothing about it; the money was sent to an account controlled by the scammer.

It's easy to read this story and assume that Steve was gullible, but he trusted Pete and had no reason to believe he was chatting to anyone else. It was plausible in this case that Pete may not have had a PayPal account. Steve just wanted to help out a friend. Four of Pete's friends fell for this, so with a single set of credentials in one weekend the scammers made almost £20,000. AntiPublic has almost 562 million sets of credentials. At the time of writing, Steve was still trying to get his money back and the police were investigating. The scammers were adept at exploiting these friendships for their own ends. Of course, Facebook and PayPal were also victims, but I am more concerned about Steve and Pete here and, by extension, you.

When it comes to building personal resilience, you should think of it as analogous to travelling abroad – you need some basic protection: money belt, emergency contacts, and travel insurance. I'm suggesting that as we travel through cyberspace, we need a similar 'help yourself' mindset. This book will be your pocket guidebook.

So how can you take control of your digital footprint and protect yourself, and your friends, from becoming victims? The first step is to identify your footprint; this will be covered in the next chapter.

Chapter 3: Determine your digital footprint

I like definitions, so for this book I'm defining 'digital footprint' to mean "the data you leave behind after going online". Most of us are aware both that we have a digital footprint and that it's hard to reduce – more of a tattoo than a footprint, we're told. So, how do you go about determining your footprint, and what can you do to reduce it?

Let's look first at the range of things that make up your digital footprint; it's probably larger than you think. Your footprint broadly splits into four categories:

- Your public domain footprint
- Your private footprint
- Your Internet of Things (IoT) footprint
- Your Powers of the State footprint

I will tackle each area in turn, but let's start with the public domain footprint.

Your Public domain footprint

This part of your footprint is sometimes referred to as your 'open source' footprint. Open source means publicly accessible.

Firstly, there's the stuff you've posted yourself. Everything you've ever posted. Ever. It's all out there, even if you've forgotten about it long ago. It's likely that even deleted posts still sit in a database somewhere. Facebook, for example, claims it is 'removed from the site', but this is different to deleting it permanently. Some data must be preserved by law. For example, the US CLOUD (Clarifying Lawful Overseas Use of Data) Act of 2018 required that *"Providers must preserve, backup, or disclose the contents of a wire or electronic communications, or any other records or information pertaining to their customers or subscribers, within the Providers' possession, custody, or control, regardless of whether that information is located within or outside the United States."* Since most providers are US entities, this means that little or nothing is likely to actually be deleted in any reasonable timeframe.

So, the footprint you have posted consists of tweets, photos, posts, blog entries and articles, forum posts, comments you may have made on items you bought, trips you've taken, restaurants you've eaten in, games you've played, videos viewed, etc, etc. This alone is a significant amount of data that is largely in the public domain and can be 'mined' to reveal information about your pattern of life.

Some people just overshare. There are lists on Twitter of people who post pictures of their new credit cards (yes, you read that correctly), and have even responded to requests to see what the back of the card looks like! But most of us just gradually post about our lives, and because we only post small pieces at a time, we don't realise that, over time, this trickle builds into a significant and revealing torrent of data, all of which is searchable and can be used to target us.

Let's look at an example of how this works. Twitter allows you to search for tweets by year. I can look through tweets from any person's account and typically work out their birthday (just search for those happy birthdays or pictures of cakes), where they live (tweets about commutes), their vehicles (often pictured with reg numbers), their pets (so many pets), their politics, their hobbies, their holidays and business trips. And that's just Twitter. Now add Instagram, Facebook, and LinkedIn to the mix. It's fair to say that any fairly regular poster to any or all of these platforms will, over time, reveal more than enough to allow hackers to target them with a 'spear phishing attack'. Spear phishing is a highly targeted form of phishing where the message is tailored and/or appears to come from a trusted source such as an email that looks correct, naming you, from a provider you use, but containing a malicious link. These messages can be extremely hard to spot.

DEEPFAKES

In the last few years technology to modify images, audio, and video using Artificial Intelligence has become widely accessible. Called 'Deepfakes' these use something called a deep learning network to produce extremely convincing fake media.

As these technologies become cheaper and easier to access, the cyber criminals have started exploiting them as part of their cyber attacks. Examples include fake audio messages (such as from a Chief Executive Officer) instructing staff to make payments, and more recently fake video to embarrass or extort people.

Next there is the information others have posted about you. In most cases this is you being tagged in photos or posts. This is part of your footprint that you have some (but not complete) control over. If you are tagged on the major platforms, i.e. Facebook, Twitter, LinkedIn, or Instagram, you will get a notification. My advice would be to refuse the tag unless it's something you are genuinely keen to be associated with. By accepting the tag, you are creating a semi-permanent element to your footprint that others will be able to see. Apart from tagging in photos, you can also be mentioned in someone else's post. You will get alerted at the time by the major platforms. Facebook gives you the most control over these settings and I will cover this in the next chapter. As a rule, information others share about you is useful to an attacker as it identifies a relationship that might be exploited in a phishing attack by providing a believable name from whom an email, post, or friend request might come.

Then there is information about you in public records such as the electoral register, companies house, or the phone book. This is open source and accessible. Many websites have trawled this dataset and made it available. Sites such as pipl.com, 192.com, 123people.com and many others are specialist people search engines that can identify social media accounts, email addresses, home addresses, and even mobile phone numbers. If you're a current or former director of a company then your details, perhaps including your home address, will appear on the company register (Companies House in the UK).

All of the above can be gleaned by using search engines based on your name, email, or phone number. But your images – especially profile pictures – can also appear in odd places or be used by others. It's well worth checking to see if anyone is using your picture as their profile in a 'catfishing' exercise or an online identity theft. The term catfishing is often used to describe the practice of using other people's photographs when looking for relationships on the net. This happened to Ruth Palmer[15] back in 2015. Ruth discovered that for three years somebody had been routinely downloading photographs of her, her family, and friends from social networks, and setting up a network of fake media profiles of them, which all communicate with each other.

The free Google reverse image search tool at TinEye.com will pick up anyone that has simply stolen your profile picture. Sadly, these days, with the advent of deepfake technology, a more sophisticated attack is harder to detect, but the tool will pick up a straightforward copy. This works the other way around as well! If you're in an online relationship and want to check the other party is not catfishing you, it's worth using TinEye on their profile pictures. Let's bring this all together – see Table 3.1

---

[15]   https://www.bbc.co.uk/news/technology-31710738

Table 3.1 - A simple process for searching your own publicly available digital footprint

Step	Action
1	Make a list of: • Email addresses (home and work) • If you have (or had) an unusual surname (like me) then it's worth searching for that but add your first name to make it more specific • Mobile phone numbers, current and old • Account handles/Avatar names used in forums, games etc.
2	Open a 'private' (incognito) window on your browser of choice. With a modern browser this should mean you are not logged in to any accounts and have no cookies. This is important as it will give you a true picture of what others can see about you. A guide on how to do this for each major browser can be found at https://www.howtogeek.com/269265/how-to-enable-private-browsing-on-any-web-browser/ Note: Ideally this should be done from a new IP address, as opposed to your home broadband address, so if you have a VPN (virtual private network) turn it on for this. I will cover VPNs later, but if you don't have one, don't worry for now.
3	Search for each item on your list in a new tab or window, using your favourite search engine.
4	Review the output to see if there are any surprises.

Step	Action
5	Use tineye.com in a private browser window to search for all your profile pictures from Facebook, Twitter, Instagram, and LinkedIn. If you have posted more sensitive images of yourself or loved ones, you can also search to see if those images have been shared or used by others.
6	Visit haveibeenpwned.com and search for your email addresses.
7	Rinse and repeat. Make a note of all the results you are unhappy with.
8	If these are posts or items you control (such as tags), then log onto those accounts and delete/modify as needed. The next chapter covers this area in more detail.
9	Lastly, there is information about you as a result of leaks and data breaches. Much of this data sits on the Dark Web and I would strongly advise against looking for it yourself unless you know what you are doing. Fortunately, those data breaches that have ended up in the public domain have been collated by Troy Hunt, and can be easily searched on his website, haveibeenpwned.com. Search using your email addresses to see what breaches you are in. Troy has amassed billions of records so it's almost certain you are in one or more data breaches. Again, I will return to this later.

Figure 1 below shows a flowchart that will help you determine and reduce your current public footprint.

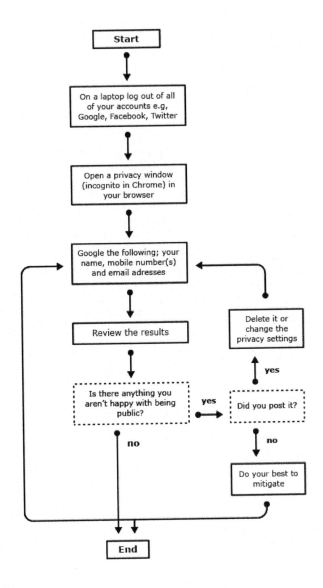

Figure 1 – How to identify your public footprint

In my experience, most people are surprised to discover what they have left behind in their footprint. I'm focusing here on what is publicly visible to an attacker as this is probably the highest threat scenario, but you should be aware that a determined attacker/stalker will take more time and trouble than a simple web search, and may join forums they know you use (or 'fake friend'[16] you) just to see information that won't appear in basic public searches. They may already be connected to you as followers or friends.

Your Private footprint

So, that's the part of your footprint that's open to the world; however, this is not the largest part of your footprint. Let's now consider the footprint that is less open but still out there. This is the data that is stored about you by companies with whom you have some sort of relationship. Your social media, your shopping, your gaming, etc. Naturally, you can see some of this data if you login to those accounts. This is the type of data that's the new currency in the Information Age. It is sometimes referred to as the Deep Web (as opposed to the Dark Web).

The Deep Web is vast. It is estimated that over 90% of online content is blocked from search engines because it requires authentication to access. In other words, it needs a username and password. Examples include an online banking or email account, direct messages on Twitter, or photos uploaded to Facebook and marked private. Search

---

[16]   Fake Friending is getting friend/follower requests from someone pretending to be someone you know. It may be an existing friend whose profile has been copied. It's a way of gaining your trust and makes phishing by sending you a link much more likely to succeed.

engines can't reach this data, and a simple Google search of your name or email address won't bring it into view.

The Deep Web is often confused with the Dark Web. The Dark Web is a portion of the Deep Web that has been intentionally hidden, is inaccessible through standard web browsers, and I don't advise you to go there. The Deep Web is where the vast majority of your footprint is stored. For example, if you buy an item online, the website you buy from will store your details (payment and delivery) as well as your shopping preferences. The delivery company will have your delivery address, and may have a collated record about you covering all deliveries, from all stores, that they have ever made to that address so they may have a better dataset than even the shopping site. The credit card company for the card you paid with will, of course, have a record of the transaction. Lastly, any advertisers on the site where you bought the item may have data about your browser, IP address, and possibly your name or email address. All of this is stored in the Deep Web and may or may not be accessible by you. The key element for almost all this data is your email address. Every online account we have relies on an email address. Indeed, email itself is a significant part of your private footprint. If, like most, you have switched your email to one of the global cloud services (Yahoo, Hotmail, Gmail, etc) then all your emails are 'out there'. In general, this isn't an issue and means you can access all your email everywhere, which is a positive advantage. But if your email username and password were to be revealed, then those emails would be accessible to hackers. If your email is hacked, you are in real trouble, so email needs the highest levels of protection (this will be covered in Chapter 5). All of your online accounts are part of your private footprint. Your purchase history, the personal details you have entered, your itineraries, loyalty schemes, phone records and messages, and search histories. If all this is well-protected then having a large footprint is not a major risk, but you don't have complete control over its security; the security of any stored data is largely in the hands of the service providers. Each account provider is responsible for part of your footprint's security and privacy. Under the UK Data Protection Act 2018 you have the right to access or correct any of this data (see panel).

IT'S THE LAW - YOUR RIGHTS

Since 20198, UK law has changed in your favour, and the obligation placed on account holders that process your personal data are much greater under the Data Protection Act 2018 (DPA 2018), which implements the General Data Protection Regulation (GDPR). You now have several new rights:

- The right to be informed
- The right of access
- The right to rectification
- The right to erasure
- The right to restrict processing
- The right to data portability
- The right to object
- Rights in relation to automated decision making and profiling.

A comprehensive coverage of your rights and how to exercise them can be found at https://ico.org.uk

If you are an Android phone user, you will have a Google account. Gmail and Google photos (which used to be Picasa) also mean you will have a Google account. By default, Google will store your entire search history in your Google account (if you have one). In fact, Google potentially knows a lot about you, including:

- where you have been (location history)
- everything you've ever searched – and deleted
- your YouTube history
- your voice searches (if you have a Google home device, for example)
- your photos
- your calendar – including trips you have taken, and tickets purchased for events.

None of this data should be accessible to anyone but you (and arguably Google). I strongly urge you to take a look at your Google data archive. You can access it via your Google account under "Data and Personalisation", where you can download an archive. You may need a lot of space on your hard drive to hold it!

Now consider that if your Google account gets hacked, all of this will be in someone else's hands. You may decide that you don't want Google to have all this data about you, in which case (in Chapter 4) I will show you how to significantly reduce this footprint.

Then there are your social media accounts. In light of recent history regarding the trustworthiness of social media companies[17] you may decide to delete your social media accounts altogether, and that's an entirely understandable response. However, bear in mind that whatever data you have already provided will still be out there, so even a deletion will not fully resolve matters. I would advocate a policy of cautious engagement where social media is concerned. While I believe that many of us would benefit from far less screen time, I do feel that engagement with the technology, whilst understanding the risks, is the best way to get the maximum benefit from it. All of the social media platforms allow you to download archives of the data they hold about you (see Table 3.2 below). They form a large part of your footprint, so I would urge you to download them and have a look.

I rate this exercise as 'two chillies' – not because it's hard to do but the data, when you receive it, can be a little difficult to wade through. I would encourage you to try, though.

---

[17]   https://www.theguardian.com/film/2019/jul/23/the-great-hack-review-cambridge-analytica-facebook-carole-cadwalladr-arron-banks

Table 3.2 - Steps to access data held by each major platform

Platform	Steps	Notes
Google	Go to https://takeout.google.com Select data to include in your archive. Go to the Download your data page. Products that have your data are automatically selected. If you don't want to download data from a product, uncheck the box beside it. If you only want to download some of your data from a product, you may have the option to select a button like List All data included. Then, you can uncheck the box next to data you don't want to include. Select 'Next step' and choose how you want the data delivered. Wait a while and you will get an email with a link.	This can't be done from the mobile app
Facebook	From 'Settings' click on 'Your Facebook Information' in the left-hand sidebar. Facebook allows you to browse the data directly, but you can also download it. Select 'Download Your Information'; it selects everything by default. Select 'Create File' and wait. You will get a notification when it's ready. A 'quick win' is to browse all the comments you have posted with public visibility and tighten them up (where it allows).	This can't be done from the mobile app

Platform	Steps	Notes
Instagram	1. Click on your profile and then click on the gear icon next to the 'Edit Profile' button and select Privacy and Security. 2. Choose the 'Request Download' link under the Data Download section. 3. Wait for an email with a link to download the archive To view once download is ready: 1. Click on your profile and then click on the gear icon next to the 'Edit Profile' button and select 'Privacy and Security'. 2. Choose 'View Account Data'.	This can't be done from the mobile app. It must be from a web browser.
Twitter	Assuming you are doing this logged in from a browser: On the left-hand side click 'More' Select 'Settings and Privacy' Select 'Account' Select 'Download Your Twitter Data' (you will need to re-enter your password). Wait for an email from Twitter (this may take a while) Click the link in the email when it arrives or come back to this page and download the archive.	This can't be done directly from the mobile app, but you can request it from your mobile browser
LinkedIn	Go to your account settings and select 'Getting a copy of your data'. Re-enter your password then wait up to 24 hours for an email.	This can't be done from the mobile app

The archive will almost always be in one or more large 'zip' files. The archive will be one or multiple links to zip files that contain your data. The number of files you have will vary depending on the amount of content you have posted to the service over the years. The zip files may contain json files. These are not very user friendly to look at (you need to use a text editor or browser) but fortunately, once the download has been prepared, you can view the contents on a browser and on the mobile app. Precise formats vary but a good unarchiving program such as 7zip[18] (Windows) or Keka[19] (MacOS) should work.

Your Internet of Things footprint

I've decided to single out your Internet of Things (IoT) footprint next because it is a burgeoning dataset and often overlooked. If, like me, you love gadgets then your life may be filled with fitness trackers, smart TVs, voice assistants, and home CCTV dogcams and doorbells. For some reason, lists like this always include fridges but I've yet to come across one. I'm aware of smart washing machines and ovens, though, so I guess it's only a matter of time. All these devices share one common characteristic – they are connected to your home network and onwards to the Internet. Even if you choose not to set up an online account for each of these devices (in many cases you have little choice in the matter), they will transmit data to the manufacturers. In the case of smart TVs, this will be data such as what shows you watch and when you turn on and off, etc. It's much the same for other smart equipment, and in many cases the data being sent will be far more than you realise.

---

[18] https://www.7-zip.org/

[19] https://www.keka.io/en/

Determining the exact nature of this data is difficult, however, as transparency is severely lacking in this area. Most manufacturers don' habitually disclose what information is being shared about their smart devices, so you have to resort to reading privacy notices to see what it consists of. For no particular reason I've selected Samsung as an example and have examined their privacy notices to see what type of data is shared. Here's an extract from their 2019 notice:

OVERVIEW OF PERSONAL INFORMATION

We collect personal information that you provide directly, information about how you use our services and information from third party sources. We use this information to provide you with services, understand the way you use our services so we can improve and personalise your experience and to develop the most relevant apps, technologies, and content for our customers. We also use personal information to provide customised advertising tailored to your interests.

SHARING YOUR PERSONAL INFORMATION

We may share your personal information with affiliate companies of Samsung Electronics, as well as with companies that provide services on behalf of Samsung Electronics. We may also share your personal information with trusted partner companies, such as mobile service providers or insurance companies, that provide you with products and services that you request and information about products and services you may be interested in. We share personal information with law enforcement agencies when it's required by law or to protect Samsung Electronics and its users.

As you can see, it is extremely broad in nature. A deeper look at the types of information collected reveals more. It's telling that the information you provide directly is a tiny proportion of the data collected overall – and arguably the least useful to the manufacturer. The underlining in the below extracts is mine.

Information You Provide Directly: <u>name, date of birth, or email address</u>. *If you share your contacts, we'll collect their phone numbers and other contact information to facilitate file sharing and messaging. You can turn off or restrict these features in Settings on your devices.*

Information About Your Use of Services: In addition to the information you provide, we will <u>collect information about your use of our Services through software on your devices and by other means</u>. *We will collect: Your hardware model, device hardware information, IMEI number and other unique device identifiers,* <u>phone number</u>, *serial number, sales code, access recording, current software version, MCC (Mobile Country Code), MNC (Mobile Network Code), MAC address, IP address, cookies, pixels, subscription information,* <u>operating system versions, and settings of the devices you use to access Services.</u>

Log information: Diagnostic, technical, error, and usage information such as the <u>time and duration of your use of Services, search query terms when you enter search terms</u> *into your device in connection with a particular Samsung Service, and any information stored in cookies that we have set on your devices.*

<u>*Location information:*</u> *Your device's GPS signal or information about nearby Wi-Fi access points and cell towers that may be transmitted to us when you use certain Services and enable the Location function.*

Viewing information: The networks, channels, websites visited, and programs viewed on your devices and the amount of time spent viewing them.

Other information: about your use of Services, such as the apps you use, the websites you visit, and how you interact with content offered through a Service.

Publicly or Commercially Available or Shared Information: We sometimes gather publicly or commercially available information, including information from social networks you use, and combine this with other information about you so that we can better understand your needs, interests, and preferences. We also sometimes gather information about you when other people provide it using our Services, such as your name and contact information when others send a message to you or share files with you.

I strongly suspect that you have never read this or any other privacy notice. Indeed, in 2008 a study estimated that it would take 244 hours a year[20] for the typical American Internet user to read the privacy policies of all websites he or she visits – and that was long before everyone carried smartphones with dozens of apps, before cloud services, and before smart home technologies.

I would advise you to make a list of all the Internet connected devices you have, along with the username you used when signing up. This is most likely just your email address but may include your mobile number. On occasion you are encouraged to sign up using your

---

[20] http://lorrie.cranor.org/pubs/readingPolicyCost-authorDraft.pdf

existing Google, Facebook, LinkedIn, or other account. It's worth noting this if you've done so.

Device	Username	Mobile
For example – FitBit	<email> or FB	Yes/No

Then go to your email and find the various welcome emails you received when you signed up. These will almost certainly contain a link to a privacy notice. If you use an app to access the device, then the privacy notice may be in the 'about' or 'help' section of the app.

Once you have your list, you can either read each policy and note down what they collect, or you can visit https://pribot.org – a free website that uses artificial intelligence (AI) to read privacy policies so you don't have to. In the case of the Samsung policy mentioned above, the site produces a more user-friendly chart that enables focus on the things I care about. I recommend you use the tool to analyse policies for all your IoT devices.

For the more technically curious, you can see all of the systems your IoT community are communicating with (and block them) by using a local DNS server such as the Pi-hole. I cover this in more detail in Chapter 7.

Your Powers of the State footprint

Lastly, let's consider what I am calling the 'Powers of the State' footprint. This is not in any one place or controlled by any one organisation, but is the data about you that can be gathered by state entities in the event that you become a subject of interest. I don't propose to get into the politics of this; instead, I'll focus on the types of data that contribute to this aspect of your digital footprint.

Mobile phone location. Perhaps the most obvious dataset that the state can see if the relevant warrants and court orders are in place is your raw mobile phone call and message data. This is the mobile mast data that every phone creates as part of being connected to a mobile network, without having to make a call. Mobile phones are usually connected to three phone masts, which allows calls to be handed off while you're moving. A technique called Cell Site Analysis can cross-reference historic call records (including voice, SMS, and multimedia messaging) with readings from the cell site masts that transmit and receive mobile communications signals. Investigators can review Call Data Records (CDR) from the mobile telecommunications providers and carry out field strength surveys. Surveys are required because of variations in signal strength at particular locations caused by distance from a Cell Site or interference from structures or local topography. The result is that investigators can identify specific locations in which individual and multiple mobile phones have been used, track changes in physical location, and identify a timeline of use or non-use. They can also correlate electronic contact between different mobile devices content, both time and location-based. This is an essential component of most modern investigations. The tracking can be performed on devices using the unique serial number (IMEI) and the mobile phone/ SIM number (IMSI). Where subjects are under active surveillance, a 'fake' cell tower, known as an IMSI catcher, can be used to capture more detailed phone data in real time.

Internet Service Provider metadata. This is the data that by law (in the UK) all Internet Service Providers must collect about the websites you visit while online.[21] This includes mobile phone operators.

Automatic Number Plate Recognition data. This is the data about your car registration number that is collected automatically by the Automatic Number Plate Recognition (ANPR) cameras. It's a live database that can be interrogated by law enforcement to identify the locations of vehicles and can be used to calculate journeys of vehicles both in real-time and historically. In the UK there are around 50 million 'hits' recorded daily by over 10,000 cameras.[22]

CCTV. Essentially, all CCTV cameras can be interrogated but not in the way you see on TV or in the movies, where any camera can be viewed in real-time. Almost all CCTV is privately owned and for the contents to be viewed, either permission of the owner or a court order has to be obtained. Publicly-owned CCTV operated by central agencies or local government are relatively easy for the authorities to obtain in real-time, but it remains a largely manual process. The advent of face recognition technology is set to change this, and I'll address this in the final chapter.

Financial transaction data. This is the record of financial transactions, such as credit cards or ATM withdrawals. These must

---

[21]   https://en.wikipedia.org/wiki/Investigatory_Powers_Act_2016

[22]   https://www.police.uk/information-and-advice/automatic-number-plate-recognition/

be obtained from the banks and credit card companies, again using Powers of the State.

Lastly if you are of sufficient interest to the state a large portion of your private footprint may be viewed by state entities if authorised (in the UK) by the Investigatory Powers Commissioner's Office (https:// www.ipco.org.uk/)

So, your digital footprint is large in the 21st century, whether you're an active social media participant or not. The next chapter looks at what you can do to reduce this footprint and bring it more under your control.

Chapter 4: Reduce your digital footprint

Can you have a large digital footprint and maintain a reasonable level of cyber resilience? I believe you can.

There's a limited amount we can do to reduce our digital footprint and as more of our lives move online, this problem only gets worse. But we can build resilience against attack, and that's the essence of this book.

Of course, one way to reduce your footprint is to leave the Internet. Many have done so to some degree by cancelling their social media accounts. But that's not my philosophy. Use of the Internet is only going to grow, and to leave it will significantly restrict our lives and opportunities in the future. I want to be able to embrace all future technological changes so that I have a rich online experience that enhances my overall life, rather than depletes it. I can't do this if I leave the game. There are initiatives underway that I'll cover later that should make our footprint less vulnerable in future; but for now, and probably the foreseeable future, the onus is on us.

Account security is a significant topic and is large enough to warrant its own chapter later on (Chapter 5).

So, firstly let's tackle the main social media platforms, as these are largely within our control. To some extent there is a matter of trust at play here; if you suspect that the Internet giants are sharing your data, then no matter what your settings, they will have limited value. But the Internet giants are only part of the problem, and if they breach our trust by selling our data deliberately, despite telling us they won't, then there's little we can do as individuals. We have to rely on regulators and legislators to protect us. However, your footprint is visible to others on the Internet, such as hackers and stalkers, and it's these groups ('threat actors' in the jargon) that I'm seeking to protect you from. The changes I propose will not deplete your user experience but *will* make using these platforms much safer.

Facebook

Facebook remains the largest social media platform by far, and for many the most worrying when it comes to privacy and security. Facebook's track record on protecting your privacy is patchy, to say the least. From its inception in 2006 it has grown to enjoy over $1 billion per week in advertising revenue, and has had countless legal and regulatory run-ins. I've seen the power of the Facebook platform for advertisers, as we used it to help track down fugitives on *Hunted*. Essentially, the basic data we provide allows advertisers to target users based on age, geography (down to street level), interests, and others. I will discuss ways to limit your exposure to advertisers in a later chapter. Perhaps of more immediate concern is the extent to which others can see your data. If you open a Facebook account today, many of the privacy settings are enabled by default. But this was not always the case, and your privacy settings depend, to some extent, on when you joined. In 2005, only your name, profile picture, gender, and network were available to all Facebook users, while all other information was restricted to your network or friends only. By 2007, default privacy settings made all information, apart from contact details, available to friends of friends, and name, picture, gender, and network to the entire Internet. By April 2010, everyone on the Internet had access to your 'Likes', photos, wall posts, friends, and profile data if you hadn't changed the default privacy settings. Between 2010 and today, settings have gradually tightened. There is an excellent series of graphics by Matt McKeon at http://mattmckeon. com/facebook-privacy/ that shows the evolution of Facebook settings in those early years.

As a result of many of the changes, Facebook now offers a user-friendly privacy review feature that can be found under the help menu (on a desktop browser) as 'privacy check-up'. On a mobile it's harder to find – you have to open the menu and navigate to: *"Settings & Privacy"* > *"Privacy Shortcuts"* > *"Review a few important privacy settings"*. This will take you through a series of settings quite quickly. In many cases you'll want to set the privacy to "Only Me" or "Friends". Avoid "Public"!

Many people are nervous about changing settings because they think they'll break something. This is not the case. All the settings below can be changed without fear. Table 4.1 provides a list of what I think are the most important Facebook privacy settings to change, and my advice on what to change them to. I have largely assumed you will do this on a desktop or laptop browser, as phones, despite their ubiquity, are too fiddly.

Note on Facebook new look settings

In 2020, Facebook introduced a new look site for desktops and laptops. Not all users have access to the new look at the time of writing. For this reason, I have retained the 'classic' look instructions.

For those using the new look, the privacy settings are more directly accessible through the right-hand dropdown as "Settings & Privacy". If you need to, you can switch back to the 'classic' look to follow my instructions stepwise. The web links provided all still work at time of writing. The setting names tend to stay the same, so a quick search should find them if they've moved.

Table 4.1 – Adjusting your privacy settings for Facebook

Difficulty rating		
Setting	**Where to find it (desktop browser)**	**Change to**
Privacy	Click on privacy on the left-hand column https://www.facebook.com/settings?tab=privacy	
	Who can see your future posts?	Friends
	Limit the audience for old posts on your timeline	Friends (the only setting offered)
	Review all your posts and things you're tagged in	Click on Activity Log to remove any tags
	Who can send you friend requests?	Friends of Friends
	Who can see your friends list?	Friends or Me only
	Who can look you up using the email address you provided?	Friends
	Who can look you up using the phone number you provided?	Friends

Difficulty rating		
Setting	**Where to find it (desktop browser)**	**Change to**
	Do you want search engines outside Facebook to link to your profile?	No

Difficulty rating		
Setting	**Where to find it (desktop browser)**	**Change to**
Timeline & Tagging	Click on Timeline and Tagging on the left-hand column https://www.facebook.com/settings?tab=timeline	
	Who can post on your timeline?	Friends
	Who can see what others post on your timeline?	Custom: Friends except Restricted
	Allow others to share posts on their stories	Disabled means none of your posts, apart from those with a Public audience or where friends are tagged, can be shared
	Hide comments containing certain words from your timeline	This allows you to filter out posts with key words. It's a type of self-censorship.
	Who can see posts you're tagged in on your timeline?	Custom: Friends except Restricted
	When you're tagged in a post, who do you want to add to the audience of the post if they can't already see it?	Custom: Friends except Restricted
	Review posts you're tagged in before the post appears on your timeline?	On
	Review tags people add to your posts before the tags appear on Facebook?	Enable
Location History	Click on Location on the left-hand column	Off

Difficulty rating		
Setting	**Where to find it (desktop browser)**	**Change to**
Blocking	Click on Blocking on the left-hand column. These settings allow you to fully or partially block users from seeing your timeline or sending you invitations. The Restricted List is a useful feature if you want to exclude them from seeing your posts for a while, but you don't want to unfriend them. Be aware: they still see your posts if you set them as public. Friends don't get notified if you put them on the Restricted List.	
Face Recognition	Click on Location on the left-hand column	Yes, this may seem counter-intuitive but by enabling face recognition you may be alerted if you appear in photos posted by others.

Also look at your profile pictures, as these are set to public by default. You can't change your current picture's audience (it has to be public), but you can change any old ones individually.

Be aware that if you get tagged in posts or pictures, you have no control over the audience settings of those pictures or posts; it's up to your friend. My advice would be to refuse tags because of this.

You should also be aware that your friends' audience settings can affect you such that if they share their pictures or posts mentioning you more widely, you have no control. You can get Facebook to alert you by switching on the feature that lets you review and approve any tags (see above).

If you refuse to approve, it doesn't stop the post but does remove your tag, and at least you will see what it says.

If you want to actually delete old posts, then it's going to be a long night for you, as you can only do so individually, not in bulk. (https://www.facebook.com/help/236898969688346). There are some third-party tools and scripts that offer bulk deletion, but I have not had direct experience, and am wary of free stuff (see later). Bear in mind that if someone hacks a friend's account, they will see everything you have shared (including messages) as a friend, so if you have shared anything very sensitive you might want to delete those private conversations; however, you can't delete individual messages. As discussed in the introduction, there are many scams that hack accounts on social media and then use friend relationships to establish trust. My advice would be to verify any unusual request you get on social media through personal contact – just call them to check it's true. You may even be doing your friend a favour by alerting them to the fact their account has been compromised.

Facebook allows you to dump all your posts and messages into an archive: (https://www.facebook.com/help/302796099745838). This might be useful in itself as an archive, but also makes searching for specific data easier, as you can use a (free) tool such as Agent Ransack[23] or your local desktop search tool of choice. I suggest you make an initial archive, search it for stuff to delete, and build a list. Then make another archive to check its gone. It's also worth checking through your list of friends and perhaps move some to the 'restricted' list so they can't see your posts in future unless you

---

[23]   https://www.mythicsoft.com/agentransack/

tag them (despite my advice not to): (https://www.facebook.com/help/206571136073851)

Lastly, make sure all past and future posts have a suitably limited audience. Just remember that when you set an audience for a specific post, it keeps that setting unless you change it for future posts. So, if you do post something that is wider than your usual audience, set it back to your preferred privacy level.

Social media is characterised by immediacy. Most posts are only relevant for a day or a week, so you can probably set old posts to 'Friends' with impunity.

One of the most controversial privacy areas in Facebook is apps. The infamous Cambridge Analytica scandal in 2018, where over 50 million Facebook profiles were harvested (source: https://www.theguardian.com/news/2018/mar/17/cambridge-analytica-facebook-influence-us-election), was as a result of app privacy. You should look at all the apps you have authorised Facebook to use, and either delete them or ensure the privacy settings are to your liking (see Table 4.2).

Table 4.2 – Adjusting your privacy settings for apps in Facebook

Difficulty rating		
Where to find it (desktop browser)	https://www.facebook.com/ settings?tab=applications	
Setting	Change to	
Preferences: Apps, websites, and games	You can disable all apps using this setting if you want to. This is the strongest privacy setting, but also the most restrictive, and will likely deplete your user experience.	
Preferences: old versions of Facebook for mobile	Only Me	
Active apps and websites	This lists all the current active apps you have authorised. Remove any you don't remember or no longer want.	
Expired apps and websites	This lists all the apps you have previously authorised but are no longer active. They may have historical data about you. Remove any you don't remember or no longer want.	

If you're worried about the historical data an app may hold about you, you will need to contact the app owner, provide your app user id, and ask for your data to be deleted. This is NOT your Facebook user id. If you look on the Removed apps list and click "View Details" you will find your user id.

Facebook ads

Since 2018, Facebook has become much more transparent about the data it holds about you – particularly where advertisers are concerned.

You now have much greater visibility and control over the data Facebook, and its advertisers, are using. Most of this is data you can change to reduce your footprint – if you know where to look (see Table 4.3).

Table 4.3 – Controlling data that Facebook and its advertisers hold about you

Difficulty rating		
Where to find it (desktop browser)	https://www.facebook.com/ads/ preferences/?entry_product=ad_ settings_screen	
Setting	**Change to**	
Ad Settings: Ads based on data from partners	Not Allowed	
Ad Settings: Ads based on your activity on Facebook Company Products that you see elsewhere	Not Allowed	
Ad Settings: Ads that include your social actions	No One	
Ad Settings: Your Information: About You	Set all to Off	
Ad Settings: Your Information: Your Categories	Remove all	
Ad Settings: Advertisers: Who use a contact list added to Facebook	Remove all you don't want	
Ad Settings: Advertisers: Whose website of app you've used	Remove all you don't want	
Ad Settings: Advertisers: Whose ads you've clicked	Remove all you don't want	

These settings changes won't stop you receiving ads (I'll cover ad blockers in another chapter), but they will prevent Facebook and its advertisers using your activity data to tailor ads you do receive. Facebook will still use your basic demographic data to target ads; the only way to prevent this is to use an ad blocker or to delete your Facebook account altogether. What these settings *should* do is prevent you from seeing ads for hotels just after you've browsed a travel website, for example. This is the 'uncanny' stuff that the tin-foil hat wearers believe comes about from Facebook listening to your microphone. Its uncanny because it's extremely effective. Of course, the main power of Facebook for advertisers is the sheer volume of users and their demographic data, and this won't change as a result of these settings. However, there are other settings in your browser outside of Facebook that you should also change to protect you from this type of advertising. This will be covered in Chapter 6.

Facebook, helpfully, will tell you which advertisers have your contact details. There's not much you can do about it (apart from contacting the advertiser directly), but it can be good to know (and a little confusing!) who has your details and why. You can, however, prevent that advertiser from showing you ads on Facebook in future by clicking the remove link on each icon. You will probably never have heard of most of the companies listed. I check this section periodically and remove almost all of them.

Another extremely useful privacy setting is the 'Information About You' section. You can stop Facebook from using information in your profile, such as relationship status or job title, to serve you adverts; I set all these to Off.

Feel free to experiment with these settings until you get the experience you want. You can change them at will, without causing any harm.

Instagram

Facebook is increasingly seen as more relevant for the over 25s, and the dominant and growing platform replacing it is Instagram. In 2012, Facebook bought Instagram for $1 billion and it has grown from strength to strength in recent years. Facebook remains the largest social network with 2.2 billion users in January 2019 (source: statistica.com). However, while Facebook has more overall users, its growth in monthly users has stalled to just 3%; Instagram, on the other hand, is growing nearly 5% per quarter, so even though it only has 1 billion users, it's attractive to advertisers, with the larger ones taking a subtle approach to make greater use of influencers.

Instagram has far fewer settings overall than Facebook, but it would be a mistake to ignore them. By default, Instagram is open to anyone, so check your privacy settings: (https://heresthethingblog. com/2015/04/28/7-privacy-tips-instagram/).

Table 4.4 – Adjusting your privacy settings for Instagram

Difficulty rating		
Setting	**Where to find it (desktop browser)**	**Change to**
Where to find it (desktop browser)	https://www.instagram.com/accounts/ privacy_and_security/	
Private account	Private; unless you are using Instagram to actively promote, increase followers, or attract advertisers there is little benefit to having a public account.	
Show Activity status	This is a personal choice. By setting this you show your followers whether you are online. I see no benefit, so I disable it.	
Allow sharing	I set this to allowed. I'm careful about the images I post so I'm not concerned if any get shared by my followers. You just need to be aware that this setting allows followers to share your story as a message.	
Where to find it (desktop browser)	https://www.instagram.com/accounts/comment_filter/	
Comment Filtering	This can be a useful setting if you don't want to see comments that may be inappropriate, offensive, or bullying. You can add your own keywords or use the default set.	
Where to find it (desktop browser)	https://www.instagram.com/accounts/edit/	
Profile settings	Your username, bio, and website link remain public, regardless of your privacy settings. Make sure these are appropriate.	

Sharing photos

Digital photographs often contain additional information about the camera settings, resolution, date, and time taken, location, etc. This so-called EXIF[24] data or metadata is stored in the image file. When you upload an image to any website, the metadata is uploaded as well as its part of the file. Most social media platforms remove this metadata during the upload process. It's not known if the data is stored by the website in some other format but the image that appears on your account will usually have the metadata removed. However, if you're worried about this you can strip the metadata from the image before you upload. This can be done by using an app, and several are available for both iOS and Android, as well as Windows and Mac.

It's also possible to use the Shortcut function on iOS to strip metadata before sharing (see Table 4.5).

---

[24]   EXIF is Exchangeable Image File Format

Table 4.5 – Creating a shortcut in iOS to remove metadata from images

Difficulty rating	🌶️ 🌶️	
Step	**Action**	**Notes**
1	Open the Shortcuts App	
2	Select '+' to create a new shortcut	
3	Give the shortcut a name (you can add it to the home screen from here later)	
4	Add an Action to Select Photos	
5	Add an Action to Convert Image	Set the Convert to Match Input and unset 'Preserve Metadata'.
6	Add an Action to Share	
7	Select Done	If you add the shortcut to your home screen you can use it to share photos and remove the metadata.

Check pictures you've posted that give away personal data, such as pets names, sports teams, birthdays, vehicles, favourite bands – essentially anything that might be used to phish you, or that might be in a security question that could allow a hacker to reset your password (https://help.instagram.com/997924900322403).

WhatsApp

Also owned by Facebook and with over 2 billion active users WhatsApp is the largest messaging app in the world. Outside the UK many businesses allow payment via WhatsApp. WhatsApp is famous for having 'end-to-end encryption' which means that messages cannot be intercepted whilst in transit and their content cannot be read by anyone except the participants. This does not mean that WhatsApp is totally secure. There are several settings that can add to your public footprint. By default, your profile is visible to everyone – not just your friends. If you have uploaded a picture and added personal information to your profile that is public.

Table 4.6 – Adjusting your privacy settings for WhatsApp

Difficulty rating		
Setting	**Where to find it (within the app)**	**Change to**
	Settings > Account > Privacy >	My Contacts
Profile Photo	You can decide who sees your photo.	My Contacts
Last Seen	Stalkers can use this to tell when you were online. It is set to Everyone by default.	Nobody
About	This is your profile information.	My Contacts
Groups	This determines who can add you to groups.	My Contacts
Status	This determines who can see your status. I suggest you select the contacts.	Only Share With...
Read Receipts	This is a useful feature is you want to know that your message has arrived, but it works both ways.	Disable
Security	Settings > Account > Security	Enable
Two-Step Verification	Settings > Account > Two-Step Verification. This will require you to set a PIN which you will be asked for whenever you register your number with WhatsApp. This includes changes to groups you are in. It's a powerful security measure that stops hackers who spoof your number from accessing WhatsApp.	Enable

Lastly you can enable biometric security so that each time the App is launched you verify with face or touch. This prevents anyone from using WhatsApp if they get access to your unlocked phone. This is important as if someone gets access to your unlocked WhatsApp, they can use the WhatsApp Web/Desktop feature to scan a QR code on a browser and immediately get full access to your WhatsApp.

There are also several settings in the main settings App.

Difficulty rating		
Setting	**Where to find it (mobile app)**	**Change to**
	Settings > WhatsApp >	My Contacts
Location		Never
Contacts	This allows WhatsApp access to your contacts. It can be helpful, but it also means all your contacts are uploaded to Facebook.	Disable
Microphone	If you don't use WhatsApp calling, then there is no need to give it access to your microphone. I do, so it remains enabled for me	
Camera	If you don't use WhatsApp video calling, then there is no need to give it access to your camera. I do, so it remains enabled for me	

Twitter

Twitter is the bane of many famous people's lives (and careers) insofar as historical tweets go, so you might want to just delete the lot (https://lifehacker.com/how-to-delete-your-old-tweets-and-favs-before-your-enem-1821062277), but individual tweets can also be deleted if they contain risky info (at your discretion) (https://help.twitter.com/en/using-twitter/delete-tweets). Again you can download your archive for local searching before you delete anything: (https://help.twitter.com/en/managing-your-account/ how-to-download-your-twitter-archive).

It's worth noting that deleting tweets from your feed will delete retweets but not tweets with comments that copy the original tweet, so it may still be out there in some form. Twitter does not have many privacy settings, but they do matter, so in Table 4.7 you'll find my recommendations.

Table 4.7 – Adjusting your privacy settings for Twitter

Difficulty rating		
Setting	Where to find it (desktop browser)	Change to
	https://twitter.com/settings/safety	
Protect your tweets	This is a personal choice. If you only want your followers to see your tweets, then enable this. Setting this will mean that new followers must be approved. If you only use Twitter for a closed group, this is ideal.	
Location inform-ation	Only set this if you're happy for your location to be published with every tweet. If you're reading this book, it's likely you don't want this.	
Receive messages from anyone	My advice would be to leave this disabled. If you set it, anyone can send you a direct message. Stalkers and trolls can set up a fake account and use it to send you messages.	
Show read receipts	My advice would be to leave this disabled. If you set it, you will send a read receipt when you open a direct message.	

Setting	Where to find it (desktop browser)	Change to
Photo tagging	https://twitter.com/settings/tagging	Setting this to off prevents followers (or anyone) from tagging you. You will receive a notification for each tag if you allow tagging. This will then allow you to remove the tag if you don't like it. My advice would be to switch this off unless you're keen on being tagged.
Discover- ability and contacts	https://twitter.com/settings/contacts	My advice would be to unset both email and phone number. This can be used by hackers and stalkers to verify who you are if they get an email or phone number through other means.
Personali- sation and data	https://twitter.com/settings/account/personalization	I unset all these. Twitter has the ability to infer your identity from one device and serve ads to other devices it thinks you own.
Inferred interests	https://twitter.com/settings/your_twitter_data/twitter_interests	You can see what Twitter thinks you're interested in. You may be surprised.
Video autoplay	https://twitter.com/settings/autoplay	I set this to 'never' just to save myself from seeing unsavoury or shocking videos.
Tailored audiences	https://twitter.com/settings/your_twitter_data/audiences	Discover what audience grouping Twitter has decided you are in. You can request the list of advertisers.
Discover what lists you are on	https://twitter.com/vlissidis/lists/memberships	Discover what lists your followers have put you on. You can't change this, but you can block followers who may have you on a list for trolling purposes.

LinkedIn

It's unlikely you have used LinkedIn to post vast quantities of risky personal information, but two things that can be useful to an attacker are your profile and your network visibility. LinkedIn offers help to lock both of these down, and tools to help you check they look right. (https://www.linkedin.com/help/linkedin/suggested/66/managing-your-account-and-privacy-settings-overview?lang=en). Table 4.8 provides my recommendations.

Table 4.8 – Adjusting your privacy settings for LinkedIn

Difficulty rating	🌶️	
Setting	**Where to find it (desktop browser)**	**Change to**
Who can see your email address	https://www.linkedin.com/psettings/privacy/email	Only visible to me
Who can see your connections	https://www.linkedin.com/psettings/connections-visibility	Only you
Profile visibility off LinkedIn	https://www.linkedin.com/psettings/data-sharing	No
Microsoft word	https://www.linkedin.com/psettings/experience-in-msword	No
Profile viewing options	https://www.linkedin.com/psettings/profile-visibility	Private mode
Manage active status	https://www.linkedin.com/psettings/presence	No one

Google

Your Google account is crucial to a large part of your digital footprint. If you search while logged in to Google (on your phone or your desktop), your search history will be saved online (as well as in your browser) by default. Location data is also saved by default.

All of these settings can be turned off, and old data deleted if this concerns you (https://myaccount.google.com/privacycheckup). It's also advisable to remove any devices that you no longer need to have access, and any apps you no longer want to have permission (https://www.howtogeek.com/279384/how-to-secure-your-google-account/).

Table 4.9 – Adjusting your privacy settings for Google

Difficulty rating		
Setting	Where to find it (desktop browser)	Change to
Web & app activity Location history Voice & audio activity YouTube search history YouTube watch history	https://myaccount.google.com/data-and-personalization	Pause
Device information	https://myaccount.google.com/data-and-personalization	If you use "Ok Google", then pausing this may reduce the effectiveness of your voice requests.

Yahoo

Yahoo was bought by Verizon in 2017, largely because it saw online content and advertising as a primary way to increase growth. If you use Yahoo, there are many specific privacy settings related to your locations and related to Verizon. By default, all are set to 'Agree'. To reduce your footprint, I have suggested settings below.

Table 4.10 – Adjusting your privacy settings for Yahoo

Difficulty rating	🌶️	
Setting	Where to find it (desktop browser)	Change to
Location tracking	Preferences >Privacy Dashboard >Location History	Disagree (i.e. withdraw consent).
Privacy dashboard	https://yahoo.mydashboard. oath.com/?lang=en-US	
	Search History	Turn off search history.
	Personalized Content	Disagree (i.e. withdraw consent).
	Partners – You will see a long list of partners that can access your Verizon (Yahoo) data	You cannot change this.
	Audience Matching	Disagree (i.e. withdraw consent).
	Verizon Media across the web	Disagree (i.e. withdraw consent).
	Personalized Advertising on Verizon Media	Disagree (i.e. withdraw consent).
	Device Linking	Disagree (i.e. withdraw consent).

Snapchat has over 200 million users and appeals to a younger demographic. The point of the app is sharing so it's been a focus of concern for parents. There are a few critical settings you should enable.

Table 4.11 – Adjusting your privacy settings for Snapchat

Difficulty rating		
Setting	**Where to find it (mobile app)**	**Change to**
2FA	Settings > Two-factor Authentication	Follow the process.
Private Account	Settings > Contact Me	Friends
Story Visibility	Settings > View My Story	My Friends or you can build a Custom list
Ignore or Block followers	Tap your profile picture/ Bitmoji icon. Tap the Add Friends option beneath your snapcode. There is a section at the top labelled Added Me. Tap Show More beneath it to see who has added you. Tap the profile picture/ Bitmoji icon of any user to pull up their profile. Tap the three dots in the top right corner.	then choose Block, Report or Ignore Friend Request if you don't know them.
Snapcode	Your snapcode is a QR code which can be shared with users to let them follow you. It's not advisable to share this publicly (such as on a tweet) if you don't want to attract trolls.	
Location (via Snapmap)	Settings > Sharing Location	Make sure its set to Ghost Mode to keep your location invisible to your friends.

Snapchat pictures are supposed to be ephemeral but that doesn't prevent recipients from taking screenshots. You should get warned if this happens, but you have no power to stop this so be careful what you send. If you regret a story you can delete it, but you can't stop snaps once you have sent them.

Tinder has over 50 million users worldwide. Given that it's about meeting strangers, it's important to review your privacy settings. Tinder certainly keeps large amounts of personal data on each user. In 2017, a Guardian journalist issued a Data Subject Access Request under EU law and Tinder sent her 800 pages of data.

First you should sign up using your phone number rather than connecting to your Facebook or Google account. This minimises the amount of personal data you will be sharing with the App. The type of information acquired by the App includes your location (which is the point), Facebook likes (if connected), links to Instagram photos (even if the account has been deleted), conversations with matches, and how many Facebook friends you have. It's also important to remember that when you're chatting with someone over Tinder, you are disclosing your information to the app in addition to the person you're talking with. Some research in 2018 by security company Checkmarx[25] demonstrated that someone on the same Wi-Fi network could observe activity on the app because it failed to use encryption correctly (see section on VPNs in Chapter 8 to protect against this).

---

[25]   https://www.wired.com/story/
tinder-lack-of-encryption-lets-strangers-spy-on-swipes/

Table 4.12 – Adjusting your privacy settings for Tinder

Difficulty rating		
Setting	**Where to find it (mobile app)**	**Change to**
Read receipts	https://tinder.com/app/settings/readReceipts	Disable
Connect Instagram	This can be accessed on the mobile app under your profile settings.	It's a personal choice, but I'd advise against connecting your Instagram account.

TikTok is the fastest growing social media start-up. But as in any online community, TikTok is not just a platform for cool vloggers and their fans. It's also a platform for haters, spammers, and scammers. Given the target audience is younger, this is a major concern for many parents. Although it's only a video sharing app, it does record information such as your location, and the only way to turn this off is to turn it off for everything on your device. Given the owners of the company are Chinese many privacy campaigners are advising against installing this app if users are members of a community of interest to the Chinese government. That said, there's no actual evidence that this data is being shared, it's just precautionary advice. TikTok does have a transparency report[26] in which it lists all countries that have asked for data. At the time of writing this states that it has not shared any data with countries not listed. This is referred to as a 'warrant canary'. If the statement disappears from future reports, it might be

---

[26] https://www.tiktok.com/safety/resources/transparency-report

inferred that a country has demanded access but TikTok is unable to declare this. Of course, this still requires some level of trust in its basic integrity.

In terms of the settings you do have control over, let's start with protecting your account from hacking. TikTok offers very few security settings. To see them, tap the Me icon, and then the three dots in the upper right corner of the screen. The settings you need are under Manage my account.

Table 4.13 – Adjusting your privacy settings for TikTok

Difficulty rating		
Setting	**Where to find it (mobile app)**	**Change to**
Privacy and safety	Private account	Private account. This means you get to approve followers. Not much use if you want to become 'TikTok famous' but definitely more secure for those who just want to browse or post videos to just their friends.
	Suggest your account to others	Switch off for maximum privacy.
	Personalisation and data	Switch off personalised ads. You can also download your TikTok data from here.
	Allow your videos to be downloaded	Set to off
	Who can send you direct messages	Set to friends

Difficulty rating		
Setting	Where to find it (mobile app)	Change to
	Who can stitch or duet with your videos	Set to friends
	Who can react to your videos	Set to friends
	Who can view your liked videos	Set to Only Me
	Who can comment on your videos	Set to friends
	Comment filters	Set to On
Manage my account> password	TikTok has no two-factor identification (2FA) setting, only the log in with verification code option. In this case, TikTok sends you a one-time access code in a text message. However, that's not two-factor authentication; the code doesn't complement your password but rather replaces it. Simply put, if someone has the code, they can log in to your account without a password. This solution is far from ideal, because codes sent by SMS are far from the most reliable protection – although at least TikTok's approach will save you if your password gets stolen; without that code, no one can log in from an unfamiliar device.	

Strava has recently been in the news (http://www.bbc.co.uk/news/technology-42853072 unencrypted site), regarding information leakage as a result of public posts. If you post your runs and rides, then be aware that the default privacy setting is public. Strava has posted a useful blog to help you lock things down (https://blog.strava.com/privacy-14288/).

Online Forums. Many people join online forums and post freely. Be aware that in most cases these posts will be public or at least visible to all other forum members. If you believe your accounts (and therefore your posts) are anonymous, then check that your profile name, avatar, and any other 'about' data doesn't reveal who you are. Many people pick the same name for all their forums and it can be easy to collate these and work out basic information – essentially, threads that can be woven into a more revealing pattern. The more posts people make, the more data there is to analyse, and any single post containing, say, an email address can de-anonymise everything.

Credit Card Data. Now let's tackle credit cards – what sites have you saved details on? If the number is large, it might be time to get a new card ... report the old one damaged, get a new one, with a new expiry and CVV, and all those old cards are less of a risk. In future, I would advise that you *don't* save your card details on websites. If a site gets breached, you won't then be a victim. Some sites insist on storing a valid card number (e.g. Amazon), so you might not be able to do this across the board. I would suggest that its highly advisable to do this for all the 'mom and pop' websites, where security may not be a high priority or where they may lack security skills. I generally prefer to pay using PayPal wherever I can, as it reduces the risk a little further. Some of my friends and colleagues use prepaid cards for all online purchases and it's a good idea if you have the discipline. Worst case, I just enter fresh card details every time I buy (and uncheck the 'save' box). My password manager (see later) does support storing and populating card details semi-automatically, so some of the typing is reduced.

All of this is harder where apps are concerned. If you do a lot of purchases using apps, it's often the case that card details have to be stored by the provider, so there's not much you can do here.

Browsing. Everyone has their personal favourite browser and are usually reluctant to change. After email, you're most likely to pick up malware through browsing, and usually downloading. Browsers are a key target of hackers[27] – especially banking malware – so the most important thing is to keep your browser up to date at all times. All browsers can have their security settings tightened to make browsing a bit safer, but browsers are where the biggest trade-offs come between user experience and security. Many of the more secure settings will deplete your user experience somewhat (e.g. disabling Java or Flash). I believe the added security is worth it, but you may not. However, it's still useful to be aware. You can find a quick guide to browser security settings here: (https://heimdalsecurity.com/blog/ultimate-guide-secure-online-browsing/). I would suggest that using an ad blocker is a painless initial step, and particularly relevant at the time of writing.[28]

Lastly in this section, you shouldn't ignore the information you keep behind your logins. You should periodically review older messages and files (say, older than one year) to see if they ought to be retained. Extremely sensitive files kept online should probably be considered for additional protection or taken offline.

---

[27]   https://securelist.com/it-threat-evolution-q3-2017-statistics/83131/

[28]   https://www.forbes.com/sites/leemathews/2018/01/26/hackers-abuse-google-ad-network-to-spread-malware-that-mines-cryptocurrency/#67ad969c7866

How to remove your data from websites. If you find something you aren't happy with during your research and it's not data you can easily delete yourself, you can ask the publisher to remove it.

Most of the things that people want removed are things they voluntarily posted at an earlier time. Under many websites' Terms of Use, you lose rights in whatever you post as soon as you post it. That's why it's absolutely key that you think before you post, because it could be on the Internet forever.

You have to have a valid reason to force a website to remove content. In the EU, you can demand that data be corrected if it is inaccurate, and you can demand that it is no longer processed (see below). Looking bad in a picture or disliking a comment someone made on your Facebook wall isn't enough. In many cases, however, even though sites don't have to take content down, they may do it just to help you out. Asking nicely can get results!

The UK Information Commissioner has some excellent advice at https://ico.org.uk/your-data-matters/your-right-to-get-your-data-deleted/ but a brief summary is given below.

You can demand data be deleted if any of these are true:

- The organisation no longer needs your data for the original reason they collected or used it.
- You initially consented to the organisation using your data but have now withdrawn your consent.

- You have objected to the use of your data, and your interests outweigh those of the organisation using it.
- You have objected to the use of your data for direct marketing purposes.
- The organisation has collected or used your data unlawfully.
- The organisation has a legal obligation to erase your data.
- The data was collected from you as a child for an online service.

See 192.com as an example: https://www.192.com/c01/new-request/

General tips

I have attempted to cover the major platforms in this chapter, but new apps and sites appear all the time, so here are some general privacy and security tips you can apply to any apps/websites:

1. Turn on two-factor authentication if it is supported.
2. Review privacy settings for your account regularly.
3. Switch off location-related privacy/sharing settings.
4. Set your visibility settings to the lowest you are comfortable with. Many sites start with everything visible.
5. Disable personalisation for ads.
6. If data download is supported, get a regular download and check it.
7. Don't ignore login notifications.

Chapter 5: Protect your accounts – The Password Problem

No book on cyber resilience can ignore the problem of passwords. They are the encrypted 'elephant in the room'.

"He's not the elephant in the room. He's the elephant that never forgets all the computer passwords."

CartoonStock.com

Everybody hates passwords. I've never met anyone who liked them – although I have met several people who were 'proud' of 'their password' (more on this later). I'm going to try and persuade you that passwords are your friend, and that good password management is the key to keeping you resilient in the online world. In fact, if the password problem *was* fixed, the whole cyber resilience issue would be dramatically reduced. I'll discuss the future demise of passwords in a later chapter, but for our purposes now, let's suppose passwords are here for a while longer and that they remain a pressing issue.

On average, people have around 100 online accounts (I have over 600). If you're one of those people who never delete emails, try the following. Go into your email and search for the word 'welcome'. Almost every website you sign up for will send you an email saying 'welcome to facewittergram' or suchlike. This search will effectively tell you how many online accounts you have. Another way to determine this is to search for 'order confirmation', although this will also pick up lots of advertising emails.

Why does this matter? Well, put simply, if you use a single password for everything then it's as though you have just 'whispered' it to every one of the businesses you have accounts with. That's over 100 strangers you just gave your secret to. How good is their security, do you suppose? You have no idea, but you are relying on this completely. It really matters because if any one of those websites or companies gets hacked, then all your online accounts are exposed to the hackers. To put it bluntly, you just put all your online security into the hands of your local pizza shop or takeaway. It doesn't matter if most of these accounts contain no data of any importance. Also, stop thinking about your credit card details because that's not what is at stake here; if you reuse your password widely then your entire online life is open.

But everybody still hates passwords, and the idea of having several – possibly hundreds – seems like an irreconcilable problem. So here are the flawed strategies that most people adopt:

1. The 'Rock Solid' strategy. This is the person who states loudly in the pub that they only have one password, but nobody could ever guess it – it's 'Rock Solid'. Really? Let's explore that. It has been shown that some websites (including Facebook) have at some time stored their users' passwords without any encryption.[29] If any of these websites get hacked, then your Rock Solid password is out there. Even if they do encrypt the passwords (called hashes), many sites don't use best practice – a technique called 'salting', which ensures each user's hash is unique. This means that the passwords are easy to crack. The Rock Solid strategy also relies on them never, *ever*, giving it away to anyone. Human nature is against them on this point. For years we were told that eight characters was enough for a password, and many websites still only ask for six (or even less). Even if they haven't revealed it to anyone knowingly, they have effectively entrusted it to every website where it's used. So, they are relying on the security of those sites, and the torrid history of website data breaches is against this strategy.

2. The 'three-tier' system. This is the person who has not one but three passwords! Wow! The first is in the Rock Solid category, used for the 'important stuff'. Then there's the password they use for lots of shopping accounts. Lastly, there's the 'rubbish' password they use for all the unimportant sites. This is a widely-used strategy so let's explore it. If you think about it, this is just the Rock Solid strategy with a

---

[29] Actually, storing passwords isn't really encryption – it's called hashing (see below), but I'm using the term encryption here in its commonly understood usage.

reduced usage, and two less strong passwords for everything else. It relies on the assumption that the sites for which the strongest password is used are somehow more secure than the others. But there's no evidence to support this. In fact, it's certainly the case that the sites for which the stronger two passwords are used will be bigger targets for hackers, so in that sense the password is under more pressure. If you reuse the 'rock solid' password across several important accounts, then fundamentally you are still reusing passwords and entrusting all your online security to all the websites where it's used. What's even worse about this strategy is that there's often a theme across the set of passwords. We'll explore this next.

3. The 'theme' approach. This is the person who states: 'nobody will ever guess my passwords because they are super strong and based on a theme nobody knows'. Hmmm. Let's examine this. In my experience themes are based on a mixture of key dates and names/initials, or dates and song lyrics/film titles, etc. People hold the firm belief that their theme is unguessable and this is the basis of the perceived strength of the strategy. Fifteen years ago this would have been a reasonable approach for someone worried about random hacking threats – although it's less robust if you are attacked by someone who knows you (such as an ex-partner) who may be able to work out your theme if they know one of your passwords. In fact, so much of our lives are on public display that working out the password theme of a stranger isn't that hard. You can work out key dates by checking their social media for pictures of birthday cakes, mentions of

anniversaries, etc. Names are even more straightforward – pets names, nicknames, sports teams are usually out there in posts and pictures. Friends' and followers' lists often give away children's initials, so the attacker has a rich source of information. Now let's suppose that one of the themed passwords is part of a data breach and is cracked. If we look at the cracked password and visit the user's social media, its usually easy to spot the theme with a bit of open source research. These are also a nuisance when websites which suffer a data breach force users to change their passwords. To stick to the theme but come up with a new password, users usually only make small changes – one or two digits typically. This means that the hackers still have a good chance of guessing the new password.

How hackers crack passwords

Most passwords are stored using a type of encryption called hashing. Hashing is the process of taking the plain text of the password and pushing it though some mathematical functions – called hashing functions – resulting in a jumbled-up number. The maths ensures that the resultant number is totally unique for every password, even if they only differ by one character. In other words, no two different passwords can share the same hashed value. This is what gets stored by the app or website. Each time you log in, the app or website jumbles up your typed password again and compares it to the stored version. If they match you are logged in.

What is good about hashes is that they cannot be 'unhashed' to recover the original password. Hashing is a bit like a cooking recipe.

Given the ingredients and the recipe you can make a dish (the hash), but if you just have the dish it's very hard to determine the recipe and ingredients. You'd have to use trial and error to work it out. The only way is to try passwords, hash them, and compare until you get the right one. When a website gets breached, the hashes are stolen from the user database and are subjected to cracking by the hackers. The problem is that computers are now so powerful that they can 'guess' millions of tries per second. Furthermore, if the password is based on a word, the attackers can start hashing with a dictionary and this gives them a big initial advantage. Only the longest and most random passwords remain uncracked, but these are the hardest to remember without a password manager.

So, if we've established that humans don't come up with good passwords or passwords strategies, where does that leave us? The only place left to go is to use a password manager.

Password managers	

Password managers take the pain out of having unique passwords for every site or app. Password managers can generate totally random and very long passwords for each of your accounts; they work on all your devices, and store passwords securely. In some cases, they can even change your password for you. I've been using a password manager for years and I'm grateful for it every day. And if one of my accounts gets caught up in a data breach, I know that:

(i) the password is extremely strong, so assuming it was hashed, it may never crack, and

(ii) even if that password is cracked, it's not used anywhere else, so the damage is minimised.

I'll cover what do to if you get hacked in Chapter 9.

To those who are thinking "but having all my passwords in one place is risky", I refer you to this article:

https://www.troyhunt.com/password-managers-dont-have-to-be-perfect-they-just-have-to-be-better-than-not-having-one/.

No technology is perfect and, at some point, you're going to have to trust the security of something. At the moment you're relying on the security of multiple website owners being up to scratch to protect your weak password scheme. With a password manager, you only need to trust the security of the tool, and it has been built with security as a priority. Lastly, password managers don't have to be perfect (although that would be nice!); they just have to be better than everything else, and they are – by a long way.

Of course, you will need one especially strong password to protect your password manager. I recommend a passphrase so three, or better still, four random words and a digit or two. If you're really worried about forgetting this, then you might want to try picking a place that means something unique to you (*not* your home or work address), and use the website what3words.com to see what three words equate to that place (the truly paranoid will want to do this using a 'private' browser session). You don't need to add every single site you use to your password manager immediately. Start with email and the next most important four or five that you use all the time, and then gradually use the password manager to change passwords next time you log in to less-used sites, adding them as you go. It may take months to get all your passwords secured ... but every journey begins with a single step.

Password managers are strongly recommended (including by the National Cyber Security Centre)[30] but they aren't infallible, and you should use the security features they offer as much as you can. This includes using 2FA (see below) for the master password and making sure it logs out after a timeout.

Many browsers now offer the ability to generate and save your passwords. Whilst this is definitely better than having the same password for every site, I would not recommend this over a password manager. It is easy to view passwords in modern web browsers and they are not available on multiple platforms such as phones, tablets, and your laptop.

In summary while you do have to place some trust in whatever password manager you choose, using a password manager is more secure than the alternatives.

Two-factor authentication (2FA)	

---

[30]   https://www.ncsc.gov.uk/blog-post/
what-does-ncsc-think-password-managers

Passwords will never be enough. Even the best managed websites get hacked and passwords get compromised, so having a unique password for every website isn't enough by itself. You could still fall for a phishing attack and give away your login details to a site – any of us can. If that's an important account – such as email – the consequences could be dire. This is why, for all your important accounts, *especially* your email, you should turn on 2FA (also sometimes called multi-factor authentication or MFA) whenever it's offered. This hooks your account to a trusted device – usually your mobile phone; each time you log in from somewhere new, you get a message with a code sent to your phone, or better, you generate a code via an app (such as Google's 'authenticator' or 'authy') on your phone to log in with, as well as your password. If you choose to trust the computer/phone you are logging in from, then you usually won't have to do this again on that device. This prevents any hackers from accessing your account without access to your phone, even if they have the username and password. It's still possible for hackers to bypass this but it is significantly harder (and in the case of the authenticator app, a lot harder). Now you're relying on your mobile phone for much of your security, make sure your mobile phone provider account is secured with 2FA, even if it's not something you use very much. You will also need to make sure the phone is secure – more on this in the Chapter 8. At the very least, you should ensure you use 2FA on your password manager and your email.

2FA also has another benefit: it can act as an early warning system that your username and password have been compromised. If someone tries to log in, you'll get a message (email or SMS) asking for a code when you haven't been trying to log in. This means that someone has got past the username and password prompt but has been thwarted by the second factor. There's no need to panic; your account remains secure. All you need to do is next time you log in, get your password manager to change the password for that account.

The process to enable 2FA is much the same for each provider (links below).

Either provide a phone number, receive a text code, and verify

And/or if you use an app (such as authy or Google Authenticator) scan a QR code on screen using your phone and enter the code produced on the app to verify.

Some services (such as Yahoo) also offer email as a means of authentication but I would advise against this if your email address is your username (as is usually the case).

Provider	Link
Facebook	https://www.facebook.com/security/2fac/settings/

Google	https://myaccount.google.com/security?gar=1 (it's called 2-step verification)
LinkedIn	https://www.linkedin.com/psettings/two-step-verification
Instagram	https://www.instagram.com/accounts/two_factor_authentication/
Yahoo	https://login.yahoo.com/account/security
Apple	Apple has 2FA enabled by default
Amazon	Your Account > Login & Security > Two-Step Verification (2SV) Settings

PayPal	https://www.paypal.com/myaccount/security/ (it's called 2-step verification)
	![QR code]

If you aren't sure if a provider offers multi-factor authentication, you can check it here.

https://twofactorauth.org/

Notable absences at time of writing include BT, EE, TalkTalk, and Sky.

If your email provider does not support 2FA I would seriously consider changing your provider to one that does.

Security questions	

Some websites still rely on you setting security questions to reset your password if you forget. These are less frequent than in the past, but they do still exist. In the modern connected world, where we all have such large digital footprints, these are a wholly inadequate tool for checking that you are in fact you. You should therefore make sure any security questions for resetting account passwords are not trivial to guess. Questions such as your favourite football team, your pet's name, or your first school are fairly easy for hackers and stalkers to determine. Remember, they may be someone you know who would have all those answers, or the answers may be readily available in your tweets, posts, and pictures. My advice would be to devise questions unique to you – or, if the set of questions is fixed, use a long codeword as your answer (after all nobody at the website checks). So, the answer to your mother's maiden name might become Basilfawlty ... (don't use that one). Be aware that many breaches (such as the infamous Adobe breach), also contain security questions and answers, as well as passwords. If you're using a password manager, you can generate random security answers if you like, as these can also be stored by the manager as notes against the website.

Unique email addresses	

If you want to take security to the next level, then as well as having a unique password for every website, why not have a unique email as well? That way, any single set of credentials will be totally useless on any other site. This is a bit more technical but is easy to do. Buy yourself a domain name – it doesn't really matter what it is, so it needn't cost more than a few pounds a year. It's also worth getting the privacy package from your domain provider that means your name and address aren't plastered all over the Internet in 'who is' listings (after all, we're trying to reduce your footprint, not make it larger). Then make sure all emails to that domain are forwarded to your preferred email address. Now you can register/change the login to new accounts with <anything>@<yourdomain>.<com (or whatever)>, and you have a unique email and password for every site. I admit this may be for the more paranoid but it's something I do for many websites (those 'mom and pop' sites such as your local takeaway I mentioned earlier). It has the added benefit of allowing you to spot where someone got your email address if you get spam or phished using one of these. You'll need to make sure you renew the domain name annually, though. There is a downside to this strategy in that your spam levels can go up once your domain name is noticed by advertisers. NB: If you are a Gmail user, you can do this without having to buy a domain. Gmail ignores everything after a '+' in an email address so you can have:

mygmailaddress+facebook@gmail.com, and it will correctly send to: mygmailaddress@gmail.com.

You can find a more detailed 'How to' guide here: (https://fieldguide. gizmodo.com/how-to-use-the-infinite-number-of-email-addresses-gmail-1609458192).

Email security	

Email trust is an area that catches many people out. Email is one of the oldest features of the Internet and it hasn't moved on much from those early, starry-eyed days of innocence. Email is an intrinsically unsafe medium. It's a bit like sending a postcard on holiday – the postal staff can read the contents, so you have to be careful what you write; email is no different. Also, when you receive an email you can't be sure that is has come from where it says; this is how many phishing attacks succeed. Because email is so vulnerable you also need to exercise extra caution when handling any financial or legal matters using email. If any bank or card details are sent or provided, you should ensure that they are backed up by a confirmatory phone call. Email addresses are easy to spoof. Call and check with the company before making any bank transfer to emailed account numbers.

Email remains the most important online account that most of us have. It's at the heart of everything you do online and holds the keys to all your other accounts by way of password resets. Every website you register with has an email address for you. Try searching your emails for the word 'Welcome' and you will see how easy it would be for a hacker with access to your email to identify all your online accounts and begin resetting passwords. Securing your email account(s) should be paramount in your personal cyber resilience strategy. The advice on 2FA above is especially important for your email (https://www.cyberaware.gov.uk/passwords).

Unfortunately, your email could be hacked, so make sure you have a backup or recovery email account that's equally secure. My recovery account is with a different provider and is also protected by 2FA and a strong, unique password. I never use this for anything else, so if anyone ever logs into it (and it's not me), I know I'm in serious trouble.

If you want to use a third-party email provider, be aware that their terms of use often allow the content of your email to be accessed by the third-party – typically for advertising. That said, there are some free providers who put privacy and security first: Protonmail regularly appears in top

10 reviews in this context. I would advise a search of 'best free email service'.

Monitor breaches and account access	

Even if you have unique passwords and 2FA for each of your accounts, it's inevitable over time that one or several will be compromised. In some cases, accounts are breached by insiders who work for the provider, so all your security can only protect you so much.

It's important to be aware, should this happen, so that you can respond. You should not rely on the various account providers (website and platform operators) to let you know promptly – they don't have a good track record in this regard. On average, it takes 206 days for a website owner to detect a breach.[31] The use of 2FA can act as an effective monitoring tool to capture hackers attempting to log in, but if all the data has been taken and sold, you simply won't know.

Fortunately, there are some tools you can use to make your life a little easier. Firstly, you should register with Troy Hunt's 'haveibeenpwnd' service https://haveibeenpwned.com/. This site gathers dumps of data breaches from all around the Internet and allows you to check if you are a victim. Furthermore, it offers a free alerting service so that if a registered email address is part of any subsequent breach, you will be informed. Whilst this may be a case of closing the stable door once the horse has left, it's certainly better to know than not. You can

---

[31] https://www.itgovernanceusa.com/blog/
how-long-does-it-take-to-detect-a-cyber-attack

then change the password of the offending account, turn on 2FA if supported, and check for any login activity that might be dubious. You may also need to change security questions and answers if these have also been compromised in the data breach (as sometimes happens).

If you follow the advice above, then any single account compromise (with the exception of your email) should at least keep the problem contained. If you believe an account has been compromised, you should inform the account provider immediately. Many of the major platforms already offer a service that checks for unusual activity and alerts you. Don't ignore these alerts. For your most important accounts there are some tools that monitor access in real time and alert you if they see any suspicious activity. I use an app that keeps an eye on several of my more significant social media and email accounts, but these days with most platforms you get regular emails if a new login occurs. Don't ignore these.

If your data has been stolen, despite your best efforts, there are still ways you can monitor your financial footprint to alert you to fraud and identity theft using credit file monitoring. This is an essential service in the modern connected world so that any changes to your credit file are alerted to you. If anyone compromises one of your important accounts (such as your utility providers), they may try to use the access to take out a loan or credit agreement in your name. There are free basic services such as Clearscore and Creditkarma (UK), which let you see your credit report. Some offer regular alerts if anything changes. I don't feel the need to pay for identity protection services, but that's something you might also want to consider. It's a confusing marketplace though, so tread carefully. I'll revisit this in Chapter 9 – How to deal with an attack.

Chapter 6: Protect your privacy online

In 2018, a New York maths teacher allowed the *New York Times* to analyse what the apps on her phone knew about her.[32] The results were disturbing. Lisa was tracked to and from home and work, medical appointments – including fertility and skin appointments – and even to her ex-boyfriend's house. The apps had requested permission to use location data on installation, and that data was sold to multiple advertising and location data companies.

Online privacy is worthy of a book in itself. The arguments around the rights and wrong of data sharing by website and social media platform owners is set to rage forever. As will the one about law enforcements' desire to be able to investigate and track criminals and terrorists who use technology to mask their deeds versus ordinary citizens' rights to be able to conduct their personal businesses in privacy. I don't propose to get into a debate about these matters, but instead will focus on helping you to manage your privacy online to the degree with which you are comfortable. This chapter will focus on those practical aspects of your personal digital life that can enhance your privacy, and areas to avoid if you value that privacy.

There's no agreed level of privacy – it's entirely subjective. One man's browser cookie is another man's covert tracking method. These days, if you bring up the concept of online privacy, you're likely to get a shrug of the shoulders and a comment to the effect that "they

---

[32] https://www.nytimes.com/interactive/2018/12/10/business/location-data-privacy-apps.html

have it all anyway". But this is fatalistic … and untrue. There's much you can do to stop "them" from having unreasonable access to your personal life. I will focus on quick and convenient tools and techniques to improve your privacy, and cover a few more advanced techniques which the more privacy-minded of you may wish to adopt.

It might be reasonable to hope that there would be laws to protect and regulate our online privacy, and there are some.

Laws that affect online privacy

In the European Union there is the General Data Protection Regulation (GDPR), and the UK Data Protection Act 2018, which interprets the GDPR for the UK. What this says, in essence, is that if data is collected about you it must be relevant to the purpose for which it is being used. All this sounds rather good, but in fact most consumers haven't noticed much of a change,[33] apart from more annoying cookie requests when they visit websites. In fact, it could be argued that GDPR has had a bigger impact on companies' approaches to security rather than privacy, due to the spate of large fines imposed by the regulator following reported breaches.

---

[33] https://www.marketingweek.com/gdpr-three-months-on/

IT'S THE LAW: DATA PROTECTION

The UK Data Protection Act 2018 describes six legitimate reasons for collecting data – consent is just one of these. Many companies rely on a catch-all reason – 'legitimate interests'. This is vague, and subject to much interpretation. The Act gives rights to those whose data has been collected. The law applies to data held on computers or any sort of storage system, even paper records.

As Internet users, this gives data subjects (that's you) the following legal rights (summarised):

Receive clear information about what their data is used for

Access their own personal information via a Data Subject Access request.

Request their data to be revised or erased if incorrect or out of date.

Request that processing of their data be restricted under certain conditions.

Request that they be allowed to move, copy or transfer personal data easily from one IT environment to another in a safe and secure way.

Request information about the reasoning behind any automated decisions, such as if computer software denies them access to a loan.

Prevent or query the automated processing of their personal data.

So, if you can't rely entirely on the law to protect you, what *can* you do?

Practical steps to improve your privacy

Some years ago, any discussion of online privacy would have focused almost entirely on your Internet browser, and we'll cover this, but since 2016 our primary method of accessing the Internet is our mobile devices,[34] so we'll start here.

For many privacy evangelists, all major phone vendor browsers fail the 'trust test' as they all track you or store your details to some extent. This is a fair criticism, as the main mobile browsers all have some sort of tracking enabled, which primarily benefits advertisers rather than you. But where mobile devices are concerned, over 90% of us just use the native browsers.[35] The last few years have seen the rise of anti-tracking browsers and search engines, which promise to be better at protecting your privacy. There may be some trade-offs with the quality of search results if you're looking for more obscure sites, but most people never venture beyond the first page of results.

When choosing a third-party mobile browser, you should consider:

- How they handle third-party advertising content and tracking cookies
- How they handle passwords for websites
- Do they enforce https where available?

---

[34] https://en.wikipedia.org/wiki/Usage_share_of_web_browsers

[35] Figures from netmarketshare.com

- Do they make history and cache deletion easy (or unnecessary because they don't store it)?
- Note that Apple mobile users are not able to change the default browser for links in messages etc.

Simple Changes	

If you can't face installing a third-party browser, then there are privacy settings you can change to reduce your exposure:

1. **Change your default search engine**. This can have a significant impact on your privacy, as search engines do the most tracking as you browse. On iOS this can be done via Settings > Safari > Search Engine. On Android it's done within the browser via Settings >Basics. More on search engines below.

2. **Deter advertisers from tracking you on your iPhone**. For those advertisers that play fair, there is a setting that can reduce their ability to track you using third-party cookies as you browse from site to site. On iOS this can be done via Settings > Safari > Prevent Cross-Site Tracking. On Android its less straightforward: open the Chrome app > Settings > Site settings > Cookies, and ensure that "Allow third-party cookies" is disabled.

3. **Clear your browsing history**.

4. **Prevent pop-ups**. Although less common than they used to be, pop-ups are usually a nuisance, so you are safe to block

them. There are a small number of websites that use pop-ups during login so be aware that blocking pop-ups may stop these sites working. I have been blocking them for years without significant issues.

5. **Fake websites warning**. Google operates a service called Google Safe Browsing, which is continuously updated with lists of dodgy websites that could steal your credentials or infect your device. All major browser vendors can use this feature. On iOS its enabled by default but you can check it at Settings > Safari > Fraudulent Website Warning. As with all things, it's not 100% reliable but better to have it and not need it than the other way around. On Android, it's turned on by default, but you can check it at Settings > Advanced > Privacy > Safe Browsing.

Location Data. I've will cover location data more broadly in the chapter on mobile device security (Chapter 8), but for completeness I will also mention it here. Many websites seek to use your location. It can be extremely helpful if you're booking train tickets or ordering a takeaway, but it's often intrusive. Location services affect apps as well as the browser.

On iOS go to settings > Safari > Location. The safest setting is "Deny".

On Android in the Chrome App, its Settings > Site Settings > Location.

Data access by apps on iPhone. Many apps want to use the data stored in the iPhone built-in apps, such as Contacts or Photos. You may want to allow this – many third-party apps need access to your photo library or microphone, for example, to be useful – but it's worth checking which apps are asking for information. On iOS, go to Settings > Privacy, and look under each area for the apps that have access. There are some strange ones, such as the "Clock" app asking for access to your health data so it can perform sleep analysis. You may think that's not necessary; up to you.

Moving to the desktop/laptop environment, the arguments are similar, although it's easier to use a third-party browser by default. There are several candidates you should consider as a better browser from a privacy perspective, including Firefox, Iridium, Brave, and of course, Tor (see below). Of these, the most widely used is Firefox, and there's a large well-supported ecosystem of plugins available. Firefox is a free, open source browser that regularly tops polls for the fastest and most private browsing experience, although at time of writing Brave is trending up. If you combine Firefox with a privacy-focused search extension, such as DuckDuckGo, you will optimise your privacy when browsing. DuckDuckGo is also available on your mobile device (both Android and iOS).

DuckDuckGo is a browser search extension that allows you to use Chrome or Firefox but means that search results are not littered with tracking technology.

It's likely that your Internet Service Provider (ISP) handles Domain Name Services (DNS) for you. DNS is effectively the postcode system on the Internet. You request www.google.co.uk and the DNS system translates this into an IP address (in the form a.b.c.d. such as 160.153.136.3), which uniquely identifies the website for all the subsequent interactions for that query. DNS is largely invisible, but it can also be a way to improve your security. These 'DNS resolvers' are provided by ISPs and can be changed in your home router settings. There are several free and fast third-party DNS service providers[36] that offer security and privacy features (such as DNSSEC to encrypt requests) that haven't yet been implemented by many ISPs. If nothing else, you may get a significant speed improvement. If you're slightly more technical, a useful tool to help you choose your DNS provider is Namebench from Google.

The TOR browser	

No chapter on privacy would be complete without a discussion of the Tor browser and the Tor network. The Tor browser is a free, open-source, and hardened version of Firefox that is configured to run on the Tor network. The name 'Tor' originally stood for 'The Onion Router' because of how traffic is encrypted and directed across different relays (layers of anonymity). Tor was originally funded and created by the US government's Office of Naval Research (ONR) and the Defense Advanced Research Projects Agency (DARPA) in Washington, DC, and has received most of its funding from the US government. Tor is well-regarded in the privacy community, and most people consider it safe to use, although as with most things it has its

---

[36]   https://www.techradar.com/uk/news/best-dns-server

detractors. The Electronic Frontier Foundation (EFF), a well-respected online privacy advocacy group, is a major supporter and advocate of Tor, as is Edward Snowden and other high-profile privacy advocates.

By default, the Tor browser is a secure browser that protects you against browser fingerprinting, but it also has some disadvantages; because it uses the Tor network, which routes traffic over three different hops (effectively acting as an anonymous VPN), download speeds with the Tor browser can be quite slow. Additionally, the default version does break many websites due to script blocking.

Finally, there are also drawbacks with the Tor network itself, including malicious exit nodes, slow speeds, and ties to the US government, and some consider it to be fundamentally compromised. Some websites also block access via the Tor network or offer much reduced capabilities. You can use the Tor browser with a VPN service and the Tor network disabled (like any other standard browser). If you use the third-party Brave browser, this comes with Tor built in.

Protecting yourself from advertisers

Everyone assumes that we don't want to see any ads, but that's not always the case. If I'm buying an item online I may well want to see what others have bought or where I might get the same item for a lower price, and that necessitates me giving up some information to the website or advertising network for this to happen. However, it doesn't mean that they should know who I am, where I live, and other things I have bought recently. It's about proportionality.

HOW ADVERTISERS TARGET YOU

When you visit a website and see an advert for something you were just looking at recently it can be slightly disconcerting. Advertisers use cookies to gather data about your browsing habits into something called your 'Clickstream'.

This is the sequence of web pages you have visited and may even include items you have hovered the mouse over on previous pages. The clickstream log typically includes the pages visited, time spent on each page, how you arrived on the page, and where you went next.

Third party cookies, although still widely used, are becoming obsolete and are being replaced by browser fingerprinting (see below).

As many as 85% of people say they have seen sponsored ads on platforms such as Facebook, Twitter, or LinkedIn. Perhaps surprisingly, less than 10% of respondents felt this to be a strongly negative experience and indeed around two-thirds of them described these ads as positive or neutral, so it would be wrong to assume that we want to see no ads at all.

Cookies and tracking

A brief explanation of cookies. Whether you're searching and browsing, logging into social media, shopping, or just innocently chatting on an online forum, you're using cookies. They aren't intrinsically harmful but, as with most things on the Internet, they can be exploited in the wrong hands.

In simple terms, cookies are just small files that are stored on your device by your browser when you visit a website or use an app. Cookies are created when you visit the site, and they store bits of information about your interactions with the website, which personalise your visit and allow the website owners to track your visit. Cookies are what allow you to stay logged in between visits to a website if you check the box. The cookie is specific to you, is stored on your device, and can be read by the web server from (when interacting with it), or by, apps on your device.

Why some cookies are necessary. One reason for a cookie is to identify you. If you log in to a website and close your browser, then open it back up, the website knows it's you because that cookie exists (it was created when you logged in). Cookies can store all sorts of information, like your preferences, your browser type, your location, etc, and this information can be used to improve your experience. Website/app owners can also place cookies from third-parties, such as advertisers, on your device.

How cookies can be used to track you. Third-party cookies are placed on your device by an advert on a web page. They can be accessed by the advertiser – including if you visit another website where the same advertiser serves adverts. This means they can log all the sites you visit that are used by that advertiser. In this way they can build a profile of you and the sites you visit.

Supercookies. At least two major Internet providers, AT&T and Verizon Wireless, inserted for a time a global identifier – referred to as a supercookie – into users' web requests that allowed them to be tracked by their internet account across everything. While both ISPs stopped using supercookies, there's no prohibition against them. Supercookies, if used, can track more than just visits by logging time spent on each site. Supercookies also get stored off your device by your ISP. As a user you have little control over supercookies, although using a Virtual Private Network (VPN – see explanation in Chapter 8) would help. In Europe use of supercookies would have to be disclosed under the EU data protection regulations.

Evercookies are an annoying and persistent type of cookie used by some websites that require specialist tools to remove. They used to be more prevalent because of browser plugins like Flash, which they exploited; however, they are less common today as advertisers have moved to a technique called browser fingerprinting (see below). Managing cookies is relatively easy to do – see Table 6.1, below.

Table 6.1 – How to delete cookies

Difficulty rating		
Browser	**Steps**	
Edge	Settings > Privacy and services. Select Balanced. Under Clear browsing data, select Choose what to clear. Under Time range, choose a time range. Select Cookies and other site data, and then select Clear now.	
Safari	Preferences > Privacy. Check Prevent cross-site tracking. I don't recommend that you choose the option to Block all cookies, as this will probably affect behaviour on most websites. Click Manage Website Data to see a list of all sites that have stored cookies, and manually choose which sites you want to delete cookies for or Remove All.	
Chrome (and Brave)	Access the menu in the upper-right corner of the Chrome window and select More tools > Clear browsing data. Choose which browsing data you want cleared. If it's just cookie data, deselect the other two options. Use the Advanced tab if you want to select a date range from which to clear browsing data. To manage cookie data going forward, go to Chrome's Settings > Advanced > Site Settings > Cookies, where you can choose how cookie data is saved, including making Block and Allow lists for particular sites.	

Firefox	Select the Firefox menu. From there, select Options and then Privacy & Security.
	Under Enhanced Tracking Protection I recommend you use Strict as Firefox offers a simple 'shield' toggle on the address bar to turn protection off for a site if it breaks.
	Scroll to the section on Cookies and Site Data, where you can select the Clear Data option to remove all cookies.
	You can also choose the option to Manage Data, which shows you a complete list of your stored cookies, which you can selectively delete or Remove All; the Exceptions option lets you set up lists to block or allow.

Cookies do have benefits, so turning off all cookies is probably going to spoil your experience. One benefit is that for websites that you visit often, where you need to log in, cookies (formally session cookies) make it so you don't have to sign in every time. A cookie can also track a visitor's preferences to show them websites that might interest them. Cookies and their ability to store user habits make more websites free to use without any type of payment. Some of these benefits to advertisers and website owners are detrimental to user privacy, however. A good general rule of thumb is to disable all third-party cookies (as described above) but to allow first party cookies. Modern browsers such as Safari, Firefox, and Brave disable third-party cookies by default. Chrome, Internet Explorer (IE), and Edge still allow them.

Browser fingerprinting

Rather than rely on cookies, many websites make use of a technique called browser fingerprinting. Browser fingerprinting is an extremely accurate method of identifying unique browsers and tracking online activity. Whenever you connect to the Internet on your laptop or smartphone, your device will hand over a set of specific data to the receiving server, including the browser type and version, as well as your operating system, active plugins, time zone, language, screen resolution, and various other active settings. These are necessary for the service provider to be able to present information in a way that will work with your device. However, the combination of these items can produce a unique 'fingerprint' that identifies your device every time you visit that website using that device. This effectively allows you to be tracked – possibly anonymously. A piece of research[37] in 2017 published by the Electronic Freedom Foundation, a respected privacy lobbyist, shows that fingerprinting can narrow a browser down to one in almost 300,000. All of this information does not necessarily reveal exactly who you are, your name and/or home address, but it's incredibly valuable for advertising purposes, as companies can use it to target certain groups. Once you log in to a site from that device, they can correlate the device fingerprint with you as an individual and target you based on observed browsing by your associated fingerprint(s). Mission accomplished.

You can view your browser fingerprint by visiting https://amiunique. org/. In my case, both from my phone and my laptop, my fingerprint was totally unique making me easy to track by websites I visit. So how can this be avoided? It's difficult to defeat this type of tracking without resorting to more risk-averse technology, such as the Tor browser already discussed above.

---

[37] https://panopticlick.eff.org/static/browser-uniqueness.pdf

Ad blockers

Ads can be annoying. I suspect all of us fast forward through ad breaks in TV programmes we have recorded, so wouldn't it be nice to skip them in our online experience? The problem is that much of the Internet is paid for by advertising, so blocking ads is really biting the hand that feeds. There's a conflict between wanting unfettered access whilst not wanting the inevitable cascade of adverts. Whole books are dedicated to this topic, so I won't attempt to cover it here. I will focus instead on the security and privacy aspects of online ads.

Most online ads don't present a security threat. However, there has been a spate of website attacks recently that compromised the third-party advertising mechanisms used by the website to plant malicious code and then steal credit card data as it was entered. Ad blocking has therefore become a desirable feature of good online security. This has fuelled development of ad blocking technology and resulted in a virtual pitched battle between websites detecting and blocking ad blockers, and ad blockers becoming stealthier. There are numerous settings and tools you can use to reduce, or even remove, ads from your online experience.

Several browsers support ad blocking plugins that attempt to block ads on pages you visit. In 2015, Apple announced that they would directly support ad blocking in their iOS Safari browser.

Ad blocker arms race: the move and counter-move between advertisers and ad blockers has become an arms race. Many websites now detect ad blockers and require them to be disabled before continuing to browse. For the more risk averse, there are other solutions on the home network that can largely get around this problem. These block all content from specific domains by blocking the original DNS request to those domains. I'm not going to cover all the options, as they range from solutions built into home routers, through network devices such as the Pi-hole (using a Raspberry Pi), and commercial software for individual devices. In my view, this battle is unproductive and fails to recognise that the Internet currently works largely through ad funding. Alternative models have been proposed which change the dynamic. The Brave browser has a model that encourages users to allow 'Acceptable Ads', and rewards users with tokens for doing so. Tokens can be donated anonymously. This seems to me to be a better, more positive, approach, which drives co-operative behaviours.

In recent years we've become resigned to trading our privacy and the security of our personal data for the speed, accessibility, and convenience of digital products and services. However, this is beginning to change, and consumers are starting to demand more accountability and control.

Sir Tim Berners Lee, a founding father of the web, has proposed a radical rethink of the current model, whereby the funding model for the web could be reshaped using his SOLID concept.[38] This means that all personal data is stored permanently by the users – the data owners – in encrypted storage (call PODs). PODs are like secure USB sticks for the web, which users can access from anywhere. Users decide which things apps and people can see. The concept is that users grant permission for service providers to access (but not copy)

---

[38]   https://solid.inrupt.com/

certain data in a POD. This might involve a financial reward from the service provider to the user. The user can see all access (similar to a credit report) and can grant or remove access at any time. At the time of writing this remains at a proof-of-concept stage, and time will tell if it succeeds or spawns a range of other models.

Using 'incognito' mode: all major web browsers support some sort of 'privacy' or 'incognito' mode that anonymises your browsing experience to some degree. Many users believe that using this mode completely anonymises their Internet use, but this is not the case. Firstly, browsing history is maintained while the browser is active (you can hit the 'back' button to prove this). Provided the browser is closed down properly this should be deleted, but if the browser crashes, some aspects of your history may be left behind. Cookies are still written by websites you visit but they will not be able to interact with the cookies you create on the normal browser mode, so that provides some anonymity. Techniques like browser fingerprinting that are used by the websites you visit will still work to some degree, even if you use a privacy mode. Indeed, every site you interact with – especially if you log in – will be able to keep records of that interaction, including the IP address you are coming from. Secondly, even if you use privacy mode, your ISP will still record every site you visit as a legal obligation under the 2016 Investigatory Powers Act.

So, given these limitations, what is the most anonymous browsing experience you can have?

Firstly, if you use a VPN this will 'hide' your real IP address. Of course, the VPN provider may be subject to the same laws as your broadband

ISP, so all this may be doing is moving the problem but at least your home IP address will not be revealed while you browse. Your ISP will be aware that you have connected to a VPN service but not what you browse via that service. Obviously, you have to trust your VPN provider's anonymity and privacy claims. Then using the Tor browser will add a further layer of obfuscation. Tor does slow down your browsing experience quite a bit, though.

It goes without saying that none of this anonymity is worth anything if you log into any of your accounts.

File Converter Services

Finally in this chapter, I want to mention so-called free file converter services that we often need for video, photos, and documents. Online file converters require you to upload your file onto their server, and then download the converted file few minutes later. Of course, all online converters claim high levels of safety and reliability. "Don't worry, we'll delete your files as soon as your conversion is finished." However, I'd take such claims with a large pinch of salt. The privacy issue is especially important if you're working with sensitive and private design files or files containing your personal data. Furthermore, using them exposes you to the possibility of downloading viruses and trojans onto your computer. Be especially wary if the website asks for your email address. That opens you up to spam and phishing emails from whoever they sell your details to.

You can use these online converters if you can afford to have your file seen by others and you have good antivirus protection, otherwise I recommend you avoid them. There are often open source software packages that do the same thing and are less likely to cause you any privacy issues. Again, I suggest you search for independent reviews before installing.

Chapter 7: Secure your home against cyber attack

The old saying goes that an Englishman's home is his castle, but for many of us our home networks offer little or no security. There's been a huge increase in the number and variety of devices we have on our home networks. Basically, the more equipment that gets added to the network, the greater the risk.

In November 2019, a Seattle couple (Jo and John) were called up to their daughter's room where she told them a 'voice' was talking to her. It transpired that a camera that had been a gift and was used as a baby monitor had been accessed by an unknown hacker who was speaking to the child, as well as being able to see them through the camera. The couple had noticed unusual movement of the camera previously but hadn't realised it was being remotely controlled. There have been numerous other similar stories related to cameras, but our home networks are chock-full of Internet-connected devices. Let's consider a fairly typical home network …

Firstly, there's the broadband router, which is also usually the Wi-Fi

Then, perhaps, some games consoles

A laptop or tablet, perhaps several

Perhaps a desktop or two?

All the mobile phones in the house – including those belonging to regular visitors

A Smart TV?

A wireless music system?

Home assistants such as Amazon Echo or Google Home?

How about your central heating?

Smart plugs?

Burglar alarm?

CCTV?

Smart bulbs?

Some toys?

Smart white goods?

An energy monitor?

A robot vacuum cleaner?

An exercise bike? ...

This list will only get longer, and in the next couple of years is set to include medical devices – both in our homes and in our bodies, smart cookers, smart washing machines, and no doubt things we haven't even thought of yet.

There are several apps that can 'discover' all devices on your home network; indeed, your router may already offer this facility. The app I use is called 'fing', and its free on all the main app stores. I've also bought a 'fing box' that monitors my home network 24x7, but the app will do a good job of identifying all your devices without the box. Its major use is to alert me when something new joins the network.

Let's categorise the above list and consider each major category from a security perspective.

The router

This is probably supplied by your broadband provider, although I've bought mine. It's the most important piece of kit on your network because it controls everything. In most cases, everything that connects to your network asks this device for an IP address – this is the unique 'digital postcode' for every piece of equipment on your network – and it also determines the naming service (or DNS). The naming service matters because when you type www.microsoft.com in your browser, it decides where to send you. If the router gets hacked, then changing the DNS means that everything on your network can be 'duped' into communicating with the hacker's systems. All traffic can be intercepted and modified. From a security perspective, 'routers matter' and they don't have a good track record. Your router will also likely control your home Wi-Fi network. More on this shortly. Routers are usually controlled by a web service you access through your browser. Many come with a default password, often on a sticker on the device; this is the first thing you must change (see Table 7.1 below).

Table 7.1 – How to change your router's default password

Difficulty rating	
Provider	Where to find it (desktop browser)
Sky	https://www.sky.com/help/articles/ turning-off-remote-management-on-your-sky-hub
Virgin	https://www.virginmedia.com/help/ virgin-media-hub-changing-password
BT	http://bt.custhelp.com/app/answers/detail/a_id/10990/~/ how-can-i-set-up-or-change-the-admin-password- on-my-bt-hub%3F

TalkTalk	https://community.talktalk.co.uk/t5/Articles/ Change-your-router-admin-password/ta-p/2204673
Plusnet	https://www.plus.net/help/broadband/router-user-guides/

I have seen several homes where the router was positioned on a windowsill with the sticker showing the password facing the window. Anyone could simply copy the information and get access to the network. If you change the defaults, then this isn't an issue (but cover the sticker anyway). If your router offers security features such as anti-virus, then turn them on.

Wi-Fi

All of this equipment is probably sitting on your home Wi-Fi network. Your Wi-Fi network is broadcasting to your street. That's the next thing to lock down. Your router password and Wi-Fi password may be one and the same, but this is often not the case. Again, you should change both the name of the network and the password from the ones on the sticker. Changing the Wi-Fi network name has a number of advantages:

1. It's less obvious who your broadband provider is (for example BT call their devices BTHub-xxxx)
2. Any guest mobile devices connecting to the network will find the name more easily in a crowded list of your neighbours' networks.

I would advise that you choose a fairly innocuous name, but many can't resist the temptation to call their network something amusing such as "LAN of Milk and Honey", "Pretty Fly for a Wi-Fi", or my personal favourite "The Promised LAN"!

Your Wi-Fi network extends outside your property (unless you are very rich and have a lot of land), so neighbours will see the name. This also means they might try to hack it. Any Wi-Fi network can be hacked given enough time but having a long network password makes it much harder. Your home network may already be known. There's a website called wigle.net that crowd sources Wi-Fi networks and their locations. You can visit the site and check your network name (I'll cover this topic again in travel security).

Another feature that many Wi-Fi routers offer is called 'Wi-Fi Protected Setup' or WPS. Despite the reassuring name, this is actually a massive weak spot in your security and can easily be hacked. If your router supports it, you should find the setting and disable it. WPS relies on a PIN that can be 'brute forced' by hackers in a surprisingly short time (a few seconds). All WPS really does is allow you to connect to Wi-Fi more easily. If you create a long passphrase (not the same as the network name) that you can easily remember, you should be able to connect just as fast. And this is only an issue the first time – when you've connected a device once, you shouldn't have to do it again. WPS is awfully risky for a feature that offers such a small benefit. If your router doesn't let you disable WPS, then consider getting a new router.

If someone does hack your home Wi-Fi what can they do? Well, if they also hack your home router, they can snoop on everything going on in the house and decide where Internet requests actually go by changing your DNS. This means they can redirect legitimate sites to malicious ones.

Now, what do you do when guests come to the house – just give them your Wi-Fi password? What about your kids' friends? Really? Not a good idea. Would you give them a house key? No? Then why are you giving them your Wi-Fi password?

Many modern Wi-Fi routers offer a guest network feature. This is an excellent idea, as these networks typically isolate users from systems on your main network. However, I would still recommend you give it a decent passphrase (not the same as the main network), just to stop neighbours from stealing your broadband to stream movies or play games (or use your connection to do something dodgy).

Table 7.2 – How to secure your Wi-Fi settings

Difficulty rating	
Step 1	Change the default network name on your home Wi-Fi network.
Step 2	Change the default password on your home Wi-Fi. Of course, if you have dozens of devices, then this will be a nuisance but it's worth it.
Step 3	Disable Wi-Fi Protected Setup (WPS).
Step 4	Use the guest Wi-Fi feature (but give it a passphrase).

Mobile devices

All your mobile devices will connect to your home Wi-Fi. I have covered their security elsewhere, but it's worth reiterating the importance of having at least a six-digit PIN *and* ensuring that security updates are installed automatically on all mobile devices.

Desktops and laptops

These are often the devices that you use the most, after the phones. They're also the most susceptible to security issues such as malware. By far the most important security settings to apply on all desktops and laptops, irrespective of the make, are:

1. Have a strong password (or biometric)
2. Make sure updates are installed automatically
3. Use an Internet security package

You should certainly use an Internet security package. The built-in ones, such as Windows Defender in Windows 10, generally perform well in independent reviews so there's no need to spend money on a commercial package for basic protection. Even if you are a Mac user, you should have malware detection software. The old myth about not needing it for Macs is just that – old and a myth.

MIRAI BOTNET

Between August and October 2016, millions of web cameras and other devices in homes worldwide were infected with malware called Mirai (Japanese for "the future", 未来). This made the cameras join a 'botnet' – a huge network of devices that could

be directed by a hacker called a 'bot herder'. These cameras were then all instructed to launch a range of attacks against targets of the hacker's choice. When millions of devices do this simultaneously it's called a Distributed Denial of Service (DDOS) attack.

In December 2017, Paras Jha, a student, and his associates pleaded guilty to crimes related to the Mirai attacks and were sentenced to 2,500 hours of community service, six months home confinement, and ordered to pay $8.6 million in restitution. But by then the code was in the wild, and being used as building blocks for further botnets.

Smart equipment

This category covers all of the other 'stuff' on your network – the home assistants, TVs, cookers, fridges, etc. This is the category that's growing incredibly fast and it's also the group that will most likely make your home network vulnerable in future. These devices are often called 'smart' devices but if they are smart, they are rarely secure. The Internet of Things is still lacking security standards, and for many products low prices ensure widespread adoption. For this reason, security is usually not something that is designed in.

All of this smart equipment connects to your Wi-Fi network, often accessed via a mobile app. They all communicate to the app through a service provider on the Internet – often the vendor. The service provider in turn stores the data and offers it to you via an app, which you log in to access, as shown in Figure 2. Provided the smart device uses secure communications and doesn't share your Wi-Fi credentials with the vendor, there's nothing fundamentally wrong with this architecture from a security perspective, although clearly much of the security relies on the service provider and some devices (such as Amazon Echo) do share credentials. Cheaper devices may also not use secure communications. If the vendors are hacked, then potentially all the smart equipment communicating to them can be hacked as well. If all the TVs in the world from a particular manufacturer suddenly start showing the same video, then we will know it's all over …

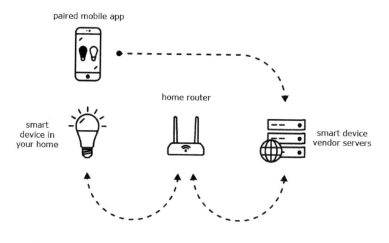

paired mobile app

home router

smart device in your home

smart device vendor servers

Figure 2 – How IoT devices communicate

Of course, the benefits to you of being able to see what's in your fridge or keep an eye on your dog while you're at work is nothing compared to the benefits to the manufacturers of getting all the data from every fridge installed worldwide. For TVs this can include viewing habits; for music systems, listening habits; and potentially much, much more.

UPnP

To help users easily set up new connections, IoT devices such as network printers, home media players, and Smart TVs use a feature called Universal Plug and Play (UPnP).

If the IoT device is behind a UPnP-aware router (most modern broadband routers are), it can request the router to allow certain traffic through to them from the Internet.

UPnP eliminates the hassle of configuring devices on first connection, and adds an element of quick information sharing. But it also opens up a 'backdoor' to your home network, which can be exploited by hackers and automated 'bots'.

All of this traffic goes through your home router (it's the only way out of your network), so it's possible to monitor which devices talk to which manufacturers. You can install a device called a Pi-hole which can do this (more later), but there has been some research on this which found that many devices overshare data with their manufacturers. In the case of Smart TVs, researchers found[39] that detailed data about every show played on the TV – including cable, over-the-air broadcasts, streaming services, and even DVDs and Blu-ray discs – was sent to the TV manufacturer or one of its business partners, or both. If you're happy to dive into the technical waters, there are things you can do to keep all smart devices away from desktops, laptops, and phones (for example, by having a dedicated wireless network just for smart devices). You can also

---

[39]   https://www.consumerreports.org/televisions/samsung-roku-smart-tvs-vulnerable-to-hacking-consumer-reports-finds/

use a device such as the Pi-hole to block the devices from access to some websites, but the fact is that once you introduce these to your network, your risk goes up and your privacy goes down.

There are some essential things you should do with every smart device; see Table 7.3 below.

Table 7.3 – How to increase the security of your smart devices

To Do	Difficulty rating
Change any default passwords that the device comes with to something unique and strong (write these down).	
Make sure the device is running the most up-to-date software version. Ideally this will be an automated feature that you can enable but if not, then make sure you check fairly regularly.	
Many cheaper devices use a technique called UPnP to change your router settings and allow access to the device from the Internet. This can lead to compromise, so turn off UPnP in your router settings. You can check if you're 'leaking' UPnP backdoors using the free tool (you should access it from your home network) at: https://badupnp.benjojo.co.uk/ However, some devices rely on UPnP to get updates, meaning that UPnP is a double-edged sword.	

Making sure this is all secure is no easy task, but you should invest some time when installing these devices to make sure that at the very least:

1. You change the default password.

2. You make sure any app or web-based cloud access has a strong, unique password and, if supported, two-factor authentication.

3. Where possible (i.e. your router supports it), connect the smart device via a 'guest' Wi-Fi network rather than your main Wi-Fi.

Home assistants

Amazon Echo is the most popular home assistant, followed by Google Home and Apple HomePod. Before getting into detail, I want to reiterate the importance of having strong security for the Amazon/Google/Apple accounts that underpin your home assistant. Anyone with access to your account can listen to, share, or delete your home assistant voice-recording history. This includes family members who order items under the same username, but your information might also be vulnerable to hackers who obtain your password.

The commands you give your assistant – arming your security system, requesting directions and commute times, or calling friends – can provide hackers or stalkers with valuable information about your daily life, which can put your personal safety, and that of your home and family, at risk. Just as you would with any other login, follow good password hygiene recommendations and turn on 2FA.

Table 7.4 - Maximising security for Alexa/Echo

To Do	Difficulty rating
Alexa. Privacy settings https://www.amazon.co.uk/hz/mycd/myx#/home/alexaPrivacy/helpAlexa You can restrict Amazon from reviewing a proportion of your voice recordings in the Privacy Settings section of the Alexa site (login to alexa.amazon.co.uk)	🌶
Voice history. Login to alexa.amazon.co.uk to view your Alexa settings. From here you can delete your voice history, but you can't stop the history from building up so this will have to be done regularly. I do it monthly. Deleting all old recordings can degrade the Echo's performance slightly because it uses your history to improve responses over time, and it will have to relearn patterns if information is lost. If you don't want to mass-delete all recordings, just remove more sensitive material. It's essentially the same as clearing the web history in a web browser.	🌶
Wake word. You can change the 'wake word' from the default 'Alexa', but I found the alternatives are actually worse at detecting false commands, so I have left mine alone. I look forward to the day when you can define a bespoke wake word as this will improve security. If you do decide to change the wake word, you have to do it separately for each Echo you own.	🌶

Table 7.5 - Maximising security for Google Home

To Do	Difficulty rating
Voice match. Unlike Amazon Alexa, Google Home has a feature known as 'Voice match' that learns your voice over time. This means that not only can you tailor Google Home to answer your questions in a personalised way, but you can also stop third-parties and unauthorised strangers from using Google Home's voice functionality to access sensitive information. You can enable Voice match by navigating to your Google Home app and setting it up. You will have to train Google Home by talking to it, but this doesn't take too long. When Voice match is enabled, only authorised voices will be able to activate the device.	
Manage recordings. You do this through your Google account at https://myactivity.google.com/myactivity As with Alexa, be aware of what personal data or pattern of life is contained in these recordings, and prune according to your appetite. You can delete everything. Google now lets you set an auto-delete of your activity on some of its services. It has rolled this out for location history and web and app activity; eventually, you'll be able to use the steps below to delete Voice & Audio Activity.	
Wake word. Google Assistant responds to two 'wake words': "Ok Google" and "Hey Google". Unfortunately, you can't change it from these two phrases at the moment.	

Table 7.6 – Maximising security for Apple HomePod

To Do	Difficulty rating
Apple's policy states that they will not use information about users' activities for advertising or tracking purposes. HomePod uses Siri and does not (any longer) make your recorded instructions available to review.	
Wake word. You can tell Siri to call you by whatever name you wish by adjusting your settings. At present you cannot change the HomePod's wake word.	🌶

As with other Internet of Things devices its worth considering connecting them to a separate Wi-Fi network if you have one available.

More Extreme Privacy	🌶🌶🌶

Bear in mind that your Internet Service Provider (ISP) must keep a copy of every website visited as part of its obligations under the Investigatory Powers Act (2016). This means that even if you use 'private' or 'incognito' mode, there will still be a record of you visiting a website held by your ISP. If this bothers you, you need to look at technologies that offer more privacy.

Virtual Private Networks (VPNs) can help.[40] You can set VPN apps up on each device where you want privacy and log into your preferred

---

[40] I provide a full discussion of VPNs in Chapter 8

VPN provider, or you can put your entire home network behind a VPN concentrator. At the time of writing there are very few off-the-shelf options here, so you will likely need to look at flashing an old router with the latest DD-WRT firmware and configuring it. A fun project but not for the technically faint hearted: https://www.howtogeek. com/221889/connect-your-home-router-to-a-vpn-to-bypass-censorship-filtering-and-more/

Router security settings	

Do you have a modern router or hub? If so, there will likely be security settings you can enable to prevent visits to malicious websites. This can add a level of protection for your whole network but doesn't mean you can safely ignore anti-virus solutions on laptops and desktops.

Many routers have anti-virus products built-in these days. It's generally much better to have the antivirus sitting on the router as all network traffic goes via this device. However, you should also consider installing separate antivirus on any laptops or desktops as routers can't see everything. In most cases, the manufacturer's built-in system will protect you. Commercial products offer more capabilities than the free ones, but all perform the basic functions of detecting and blocking malicious software (malware) reasonably well.

Sandbox browsing	

If you typically find yourself browsing the weirder parts of the web – and especially if you venture onto the Dark Web via the Tor browser – you should probably get a commercial security package. In fact, to protect yourself you should consider a full 'sandbox' solution using something like Windows Sandbox from Microsoft[41] or Sandboxie[42] from Sophos. This means that you are effectively using a separate 'clean' computer each time you browse.

It's important to consider security when you dispose of or recycle items. This is particularly true of mobile phones, tablets, and laptops but it also applies to smart devices, such as home assistants. You need to deregister your accounts from these devices and then do a full factory reset before you sell them on or dispose of them; don't rely on the recipient doing this for you. If you leave the device connected to your account, it may provide the recipient with some useful information about you before they use the device themselves. This process also applies to things like hire cars. You need to make sure that your contacts list has not been uploaded to the hire car

---

[41] https://www.windowscentral.com/how-use-windows-sandbox-windows-10-may-2019-update

[42] https://www.sandboxie.com/

when you use it if you take advantage of the Bluetooth features. Make sure you wipe down the contacts and de-authorise your phone before handing the hire car back. This is even more important if you store things like credit card PIN numbers in your contacts list, as this may give away far more than just your name and address information.

Many toys these days come with the ability to connect to the Internet. Sadly, many of these toys have a history of poor (or no) security. The US Federal Trade Commission[43] has produced a handy set of questions that parents can ask before buying a connected toy:

1. Does the toy come with a camera or microphone? What will it be recording, and will you know when the camera or microphone is on?
2. Does the toy let your child send emails or connect to social media accounts?
3. Can parents control the toy and be involved in its setup and management? What controls and options does it have?
4. What are the default settings?
5. When your child plays with the toy, what kind of information does it collect?
6. Where is this data (including pictures and recordings) stored, how is it shared, and who has access to it?
7. Does the toy company give parents a way to see and delete the data? Is the information secure?

---

[43]   https://www.consumer.ftc.gov/blog/2019/12/what-ask-buying-internet-connected-toys

Of course, questions don't guarantee answers but if you research reviews of the toy before buying (Mozilla is a good resource[44]), you should be able to get some of the answers. If the toy collects personal information from your child who's under 13 years old, the toy company (if sold in the US) has to tell you about its privacy practices, ask for your consent, protect and secure collected data, and give you the right to have your child's personal information deleted.

If you are unable to get the answers but the toy simply must be bought, then there are a few tips on how to reduce some of the risks:

1. Change the default password.
2. Apply the latest updates.
3. If possible, connect it to a 'guest' Wi-Fi rather than your main home Wi-Fi. That way if it gets hacked it will be isolated. Most modern routers offer this guest feature.
4. If the toy wants to use an existing email or social media account, you should make sure it's a 'clean' and anonymous account controlled by you with a strong password.

There is some good news on this front. The UK regulator, the Information Commissioners Office (ICO), has published a code of practice for Age Appropriate Design[45] of online services. It is hoped the code of practice will have statutory force.

---

[44]   https://foundation.mozilla.org/en/privacynotincluded/

[45]   https://ico.org.uk/for-organisations/guide-to-data-protection/key-data-protection-themes/age-appropriate-design-a-code-of-practice-for-online-services/

Blocking ads, spam, and malware for your whole network

Many home routers now come with built-in protection for the most common malicious sites, so they will do a good job of blocking some bad traffic (provided you have this feature enabled).

Very few ISP-provided routers offer built-in antivirus. Several UK providers offer a malware protection service which will block known malware sites. If you want stronger home network security you will need to buy a dedicated home router replacement such as F-Secure SENSE, Bitdefender Box 2, Bullguard Dojo, or D-link. These tend to be quite expensive but do offer good security features to protect all devices on your home network. There is much you can do without having to replace your kit though.

Control your own DNS	

If you want to go a step further and you have some technical knowledge, then there is a solution to block most advertising (as well as malware and spam) to your network. This works by adding a Domain Name Service (DNS) server to your network on a Raspberry Pi called a Pi-hole.

DNS determines where devices on the network go to get their web content. By having your own DNS server, you can block requests for sites that you don't want, such as advertisement providers. Most websites serve their ads from mainstream advertising providers (such as Google). These are known groups of servers that just deliver ad content, so this won't affect your normal web content or searches. Some sponsored searches (the ones at the top of the search results) might get blocked, but you can tune the system to stop this if you want. The main benefit is that you can add lists of domains to block, which you can get from The Blocklist Project at https://blocklist.site/.

The Pi-hole is a dedicated DNS server that runs on a Raspberry Pi computer. It sits on your network and becomes the DNS server used by all devices on the network. This is achieved by setting the Pi-hole as the DNS server in your existing router's DHCP settings. The whole thing takes a couple of hours to set up. If you buy an out-of-the-box Raspberry Pi with the Raspbian operating system pre-installed, then all you need to do is run the Pi-hole installation script once the Pi is up and running. If you are interested, then visit https://pi-hole.net/ Be aware, this is a community supported initiative and not a commercial product, so set your expectations accordingly.

Pi-hole gives you complete visibility over every device on your network. You can see which sites are being accessed by smart home devices and block them if you're worried. Of course, this may stop certain features working, so you will need to experiment. In my case, after family pressure, I re-allowed some ads but use it mostly to block known ransomware, malvertising, malware, and fraud sites.[46]

Use a personal DNS service	

---

[46] Pi-hole is not really a security technology as it can easily be bypassed, but it is a privacy enhancer.

If you don't feel like learning how to set up a Raspberry Pi, there are solutions that can achieve similar results and offer a good level of parental control. If you take out a service with OpenDNS (part of Cisco), such as their free Family Shield[47] service, you can ensure that all 'dodgy' websites are blocked for all devices on your home network. Your Internet router sets the DNS server for your network, which in turn can determine which domains are allowed or not. The OpenDNS website provides detailed set-up guidance for a large number of commercial routers but it really only requires you to change one setting (your DNS server IP address in your DHCP settings) to get it working, but I have rated it as two chillies as the settings can take a bit of finding.

Here is a high-level set of steps to follow from a Windows machine on the home network. Routers do vary widely so your router manual will be essential.

---

[47]   https://www.opendns.com/setupguide/#familyshield

Table 7.7 – Changing your home router DNS settings

Difficulty rating	
Step 1 – find your router on the network	Open a command prompt and type ipconfig <Enter> You should see some information including a line which says 'Default Gateway' and an IP address (usually 192.168.1.1).
Step 2 – log into your router	Sign into your router's admin page via the browser, which is almost certainly at http://192.168.1.1. or https://192.168.1.1 (You will need the password. If you have never changed it, it will be with the documentation provided with the router or on a sticker on the back. This is a good time to change the default password).
Step 3 – find the DNS settings	Once in the web interface, you'll probably find a DNS server option on one of the pages. The option may be under LAN or DHCP server settings, as the DNS server is provided via the DHCP protocol to devices that connect to your router.
Step 4 – change the DNS	Change the DNS IP address to your preferred server. The setting will affect your entire network.

Of course, all this only works for your Wi-Fi and wired networks at home; 4G devices rely on the mobile provider for their DNS. The next chapter looks at when you are out and about.

Backups

One of the best protections against all forms of cyber attack is to have a good backup regime. Ideally this will be largely automated, so you don't have to rely on remembering to do it. Whether you use a cloud service or a separate USB drive (or both), the crucial success criterion is that your data is in at least two separate places. In other words, backups stored on the same drive - or even a 'mapped' drive are not really backups, just copies.

Cyber attacks such as ransomware can encrypt copies that are connected to the infected machine so don't leave the USB drive plugged in. This is where cloud backup services can offer an automated and ransomware-proof solution, although I actually use both.

Chapter 8: Travel and mobile device security

Mobile phones, tablets, and laptops are an essential part of our connected lives, and the longer we have had them, the more dependent we have become. This is illustrated by a 2017 survey that found that on average we touch our phone over 2,600 times per day! Inevitably, mobile devices hold huge quantities of important personal and financial information, or the means to access it.

Many people don't realise how vulnerable to cyber attack they become when they leave their home or office, but it's fraught with physical and cyber risk. Pickpockets can watch you log on to your phone and then steal it, or the phone could be left on a bus or in a taxi. The truth is that we are more at risk of attack when travelling than almost any other time.

Free Wi-Fi is everywhere and, along with charging points, seems to be the resource most commonly sought – especially by millennials. We all use free Wi-Fi wherever we can get it without a thought, and we assume our devices protect us when we are on a train or in a pub or hotel. I would counsel against using it – at least in its raw form. Using free Wi-Fi without any other protection is the digital equivalent of finding an open bottle of beer in the street and drinking from it. This is largely because we trust the networks we connect to when we shouldn't.

A friend of mine who is a company director and travels a lot was at Houston airport a few years ago. He was in the business class lounge and wanted to respond to some emails and pay a few bills while he was waiting for his flight. He connected to the free Wi-Fi network and carried on as usual. When he got off his flight in the UK, he found he had been hacked. His email contacts – many of them customers – had all been sent malware from his email account; all his social media contacts had malicious links posted to them as direct messages; the hacker had even purchased digital download box sets worth a few hundred pounds using his accounts. It took him weeks to clean up the mess and he was extremely embarrassed about it. All that had happened was that the free Wi-Fi network he connected to was not in fact operated by the airport but was instead being run by a hacker probably sitting near him. His laptop connected to the strongest Wi-Fi signal which, if someone is sitting close by broadcasting a wireless network, will be them.

Anyone can produce a wireless network with any name from any device. You can do it from your phone as a personal hotspot (more on this later). Spoofing a Wi-Fi network is trivial, but this combination can be deadly in the hands of a competent hacker so don't be fooled by the network name. The point is, there's no way that you can trust a public Wi-Fi network. Name[48] is no guarantee of ownership. Even networks with passwords can't be trusted if the password is written on a notice in the pub/lounge/store; that can be faked as well.

Trust is everything in network security. When you connect to any network, the operator of that network has total power over where to send your device's network traffic. Even if you use https:// for your web

---

[48]   A Wi-Fi name is technically called the SSID or Service Set IDentifier

browsing it is still possible for a malicious network operator to do you digital harm or at the very least track you by recording your device's unique identifier (called a MAC address). If you use a newer iPhone/ iPad running iOS 14 or later, or an Android device running Android 10 or later, the phone will generate a fresh MAC address each time it connects to a Wi-Fi network.[49] Not all connections from your phone's apps will necessarily use the strongest encryption; a recent survey of mobile apps from Pradeo (www.pradeo.com) found that over one in six apps uses uncertified – and therefore unencrypted – connections to the cloud.

Many people now have substantial mobile data allowances that mean they don't have to use Wi-Fi all the time. In the UK, a 4G connection from your phone is significantly more trustworthy than any free Wi-Fi network, but that's not true if you are travelling abroad. If you can't trust the network you're using, then you need to use a service while you're on that network where that trust can be reconstituted. Fortunately, there's a simple solution – use a VPN.

What is a VPN?

A VPN – or Virtual Private Network – takes your Internet connection and makes it more secure, helps you stay anonymous, and helps you get around local website blocks. To illustrate how a VPN works I'll use a story from before the Internet was invented. During World War 2, radio traffic could easily be intercepted on the battlefield so the Allies needed a way to ensure their communications couldn't be understood whilst retaining the ability to communicate quickly, as

---

[49]   This can be disabled on iOS for networks you trust such as your home network. See https://support.apple.com/en-us/HT211227 for details.

code books were too clumsy in a battlefield scenario. The Navajo people spoke a language that had never been documented and was spoken by very few. Philip Johnstone, a retired soldier, worked out that if the radio messages were simultaneously translated into Navajo for transmission and retranslated back at the other end, it wouldn't matter if the traffic was intercepted as the enemy couldn't understand it. This worked extremely well in WWII and the Navajo Code Talkers are credited with helping to win the Battle of Iwo Jima.[50] This is a useful way to understand how a VPN works, although of course it uses strong computer encryption instead of Navajo! The essential benefit of a VPN is that it lends you a temporary IP address and hides your true IP address from every website you connect with, at the same time ensuring that all your traffic on your local network (the untrusted Wi-Fi) is encrypted and therefore secure. VPN connections are often referred to as 'secure tunnels' across the untrusted network.

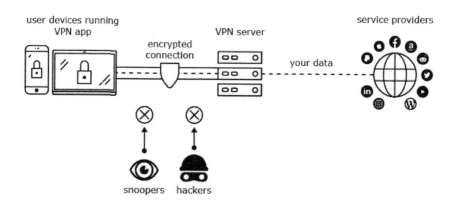

Figure 3 – How VPNs work

---

[50]   https://en.wikipedia.org/wiki/Code_talker

VPNs protect your traffic from snoopers between your device and the website or service you are accessing but if you log in to the website it will still log your access. It may think you are coming from somewhere new as the VPN will mask your home IP address so you may get prompted for additional credentials. VPN software connects your device to your VPN provider (who you trust more than the Wi-Fi provider) before sending traffic on to the website you requested. They even encrypt traffic that is already encrypted (such as https://websites). This causes a slight overhead and can often cause a slight drop in performance but it's worth it to know that everything you do on the phone is safe from prying eyes. I would count having a VPN on your phone or laptop as a 'travel essential'. I know several people who leave their VPN turned on all the time rather than just when using public Wi-Fi.

When choosing a VPN, you should consider the following:

- Read reviews to check it has a good reputation.
- Read its privacy policy. You should be comfortable with its policy on logging your traffic.
- Make sure all your devices are compatible. Almost all the mainstream products cover iPhone, Android, Windows and MacOS.
- Make sure it supports multiple protocols. The protocol determines the type of encryption it uses. Some networks block certain protocols. The ones that work in most cases are called OpenVPN (for laptops), L2TP, and IPSEC (for phones and tablets). These all use strong encryption and will work in most cases. If none of your VPN protocols work, you should be concerned and assume the Wi-Fi network is dodgy.

- Make sure it supports multiple devices. Ideally, you want to install the same product across all your devices but only have one account and one monthly fee (although there are free versions of many of the products, they often only support single devices).
- Many computer websites regularly review VPN products and will provide you with the information you need.

When it comes to booking a hotel, Wi-Fi is an absolute must for most travellers. Indeed, when asked what services are of particular importance to them, 93% of guests rated Wi-Fi as the most important service they used.[51] But hotel Wi-Fi is not to be trusted. A wireless network consists of the clients (users such as yourself), an 'access point', and a router. The router is connected to the Internet, and wireless access points create the radio signals used to access public Wi-Fi. The easiest way for an attacker to exploit public Wi-Fi is to position themselves on the network between devices and the router using something called an 'evil twin' or 'man-in-the-middle' attack. Devices will usually connect to the strongest signal for a given Wi-Fi network name.

---

[51]   http://www.hotelwifi.com/ 2019 survey results

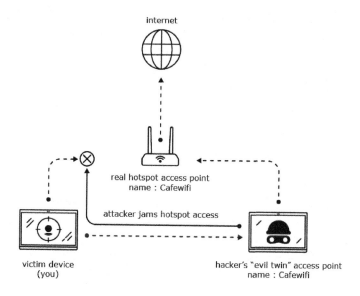

internet

real hotspot access point
name : Cafewifi

attacker jams hotspot access

victim device
(you)

hacker's "evil twin" access point
name : Cafewifi

Figure 4 – 'Evil Twin' Wi-Fi attack

When you attempt to access a website or service, the attacker acts as a relay, while also capturing and saving the information passed along. It's unlikely you'd notice anything amiss while your data was stolen.

When the attacker acts as a relay, they gain access to all the information passing from you to the websites you visit, including passwords, transactions, and messaging. Again, a VPN is a strong protection against this type of attack.

If you don't have a VPN or can't get it to work, as sometimes happens in a foreign country (such as China), or on a Wi-Fi network that blocks VPNs (which is a very worrying sign in itself), you might want to consider using your phone as a personal hotspot to secure your tablet or laptop connection, with or without your VPN. This is significantly more secure than using any public Wi-Fi network. It may be slower than Wi-Fi as it depends on the data signal to your phone and will cost you some of your data allowance (which may be expensive), but purely from a security perspective it is far safer than using a Wi-Fi network. Certainly, if you have a generous data allowance and a 4G connection or better, it is my recommended option. This is because you aren't required to trust any network provider other than your VPN service provider and the telecoms provider – which may not be entirely trustworthy in some countries, but generally not a concern for the average user. Make sure the personal hotspot has a strong password and, if possible, make the hotspot name (which is usually the device name) something anonymous.

Turn your Wi-Fi off!

So that's how to protect your traffic using your phone when out and about, but there are several other areas you should tighten up. When you aren't actually using any Wi-Fi networks you should disable the Wi-Fi on your devices. This is because all Wi-Fi devices send out continuous 'beacons' that probe for networks they've connected to previously. This will mean that your phone is asking for networks such as your home Wi-Fi, your work Wi-Fi, and any other network you've connected to. This can be detected by anyone who is listening using any wireless device. Your home router is likely to have a standard name, which is unique and supplier-specific. There is a website called wigle.net that records all Wi-Fi networks and their locations (it provides publicly accessible data for over 350 million wireless access points collected by volunteers). As you wander through the airport with your phone Wi-Fi turned on, it will be beaconing for your home network. Anyone nearby can detect that and look up the address, which they might use to infer your house is empty; a burglar's paradise. Advertisers have also been known to use this technique. In London in 2013, rubbish bins were fitted with Wi-Fi detectors which used this feature to track people. In fact, your smartphone is constantly scanning for beacons broadcast by wireless access points and using your GPS to associate those networks' unique device identifiers (a MAC address) with your location. This information is then uploaded to Google or Apple, amassing the two largest collections of wireless network maps in the world. Has your phone ever prompted you to "Turn on Wi-Fi for better location accuracy?" This feature uses your phone's wireless feature to scan and upload nearby access points to mine these proprietary datasets, collected en masse (without payment), to offer highly-accurate geolocation information that can be derived from these network fingerprints. Useful for you perhaps, but extremely valuable to advertisers. So, turn Wi-Fi off if you're not using it.

Juice-jacking – reality or myth?

If you connect your devices to anything public, be it wireless or wired Internet, or USB power charging stations, it's best to assume that these are not safe. In November 2019, Los Angeles' District Attorney's Office published an advisory to travellers about the dangers of public USB ports. These ports could be used for an attack that has been called juice-jacking. This is where the charging port is actually used to hack the phone. This is technically possible but is not known to be widespread. If you travel a lot and rely on public charging points extensively you might want to consider purchasing a USB condom –

these are inexpensive devices that sit between the public charge point and your USB cable and prevent anything other than power passing to the device.

So, we have covered security while you are using your phone when out and about, but what about when you lose the phone?

For Pete's sake use a PIN

Almost half a million people (446,000) in the UK had their phones stolen last year, but figures show mobile thefts are falling.[52] However, only half of smartphone owners use a PIN or lock code, and over one-third (32%) take no security measures with their phone at all (see Table 8.1 below). I hope you aren't one of them, or that you won't be after reading this chapter. There are numerous guides on how to best secure your mobile phone and many are device-specific. Here, I'll cover the settings that can give you the greatest security gains for the least reduction in user experience.

---

[52]   Source Protect Your Bubble https://uk.protectyourbubble.com/our-blog/blog/2017/03/23/nearly-half-million-brits-mobile-phone-stolen-last-year

Table 8.1 – Security measures taken by mobile phone owners (%)

Use PIN or lock code	53%
Mobile phone insurance	31%
App to lock phone remotely	21%
Made a note of phone serial number if stolen	17%
Made a note of service provider number if stolen	14%
Installed antivirus/spyware	10%
Placed on asset register	5%
Physically marked phone	2%
No security	32%

For the 47% who don't use a PIN, this is far more dangerous than they realise. If their phone is stolen without any PIN, then the criminals can copy or access the data on the phone. This will include saved passwords, contacts, notes, and photos/videos – arguably far more valuable than the phone itself. Unless you have a mobile phone that predates 2014, encryption on the phone's memory will be enabled by default, but its only as good as the PIN you set.

So, if you use a PIN, is the data on the phone safe if the phone is stolen? Well, broadly yes, provided the PIN is not trivial to guess. The thieves will try 0000, 1111, 1212, 1234, 2580 (straight down the middle). Most phones allow multiple attempts before any security features, such as self-wiping, are activated. I would recommend you use at least a six-digit PIN and enable the feature that wipes the phone after eight failed attempts. This means that should the device be stolen or lost, its contents are effectively inaccessible. If the FBI struggles to break the encryption, you can be confident the average phone thief can't – certainly not before you can issue the 'remote wipe' command.

Table 8.2 – How to change your phone's PIN

Difficulty rating	
iOS	Navigate to Settings > Touch ID (or Face ID) & Passcode, then after entering your current passcode to unlock the preferences, select Change Passcode. You'll need to enter your current passcode in again, then tap on Passcode Options and select six-Digit Numeric Code.
Android	Open your phone's Settings > Security & location. (If you don't see Security & location, tap Security) > Screen lock. Tap the screen lock option you'd like to use. Follow the on-screen instructions.

Pattern or PIN?

Most phones these days have good biometric security, and this saves you having to enter your PIN every time. For most practical purposes, this security technology is robust and can be relied on, but don't fool yourself into thinking they are more secure than a good passcode – they aren't.

Many Android users prefer a pattern to a PIN, but patterns are more prone to so-called shoulder surfing. I have seen many people unlock phones on buses and trains using patterns, and most are easy to recognise from a distance whereas PINs are less so. The very fact that patterns are easy to remember makes them easy to recognise from a distance, and therefore less secure than a six-digit PIN. This is where biometrics really excels as an authentication method. In public environments, face, iris, or fingerprint recognition is a strong defence against the pickpocket looking to steal the phone and observe your login beforehand.

Location services

I would advise taking time to disable location services on any apps where you don't want it. Personally, I like to geotag my photos, but I'm less keen on giving my location to my budget airline apps or the app that sends me football scores. The *New York Times* runs The Privacy Project[53] which has some excellent stories and resources, as well as high level tips on how to disable location tracking.

https://www.nytimes.com/interactive/2019/12/19/opinion/location-tracking-privacy-tips.html

---

[53] https://www.nytimes.com/interactive/2019/opinion/internet-privacy-project.html

Table 8.3 – How to tighten up location sharing

Difficulty rating	🌶️	
iOS	Go to Settings > Privacy > Location Services. You can choose when to share your location for each app.	
	You can also **prevent your phone from sharing your location** in the background: go to Settings > General > Background App Refresh and disable it. This will not affect your ability to receive push notifications.	
	You can clear the list of frequently visited locations by going to Settings > Privacy > Location Services > System Services > Significant Location and selecting Clear History. An explanation of the other settings in this section is given below. Disable those you are uncomfortable with.	
	Location-based alerts	Used in location-based notifications with Siri, such as "When I get to the supermarket remind me to buy butter". Also, it allows the Wallet app to bring up your boarding pass when you arrive at the airport. Safe to disable.
	Location-based apple ads	I switch this off.
	Location-based suggestions	I switch this off.
	Motion calibration & distance	If you track steps and flights of stairs climbed or use a fitness app then you need this on.
	Networking & wireless	According to Apple this is caused by the new U1 ultra-wideband (UWB) that needs to be turned off in certain locations due to international regulatory requirements. Due to this, iOS will use Location Services to determine if the phone is in a prohibited location, and if it is, will disable ultra-wideband. Safe to disable.

	Setting time zone	I leave this on.
	Share my location	If you are connected to friends or family on the 'Find My' app then this allows them to see where you are.
	System customisation	Your iPhone will customise system appearance, behaviour and settings using your current location, for example by automatically enabling Smart Charging when you are at home. This customisation data does not leave your device. Safe to disable.
	Wi-fi calling	If you use Wi-Fi calling, you'll need this enabled. If you don't use Wi-Fi calling, or have a device that doesn't support it, you can disable this feature.
	Product improvement	Safe to disable all these.
	Status bar icon	Useful to leave this on as a small arrow will appear in the status bar when location services are in use.
Android	Go to Settings > Security & location > Location. Find the 'Use location' feature at the top and toggle it off. Look a little further down to the 'Advanced' button, tap on it, and look for 'Location services'. You'll have four categories that you can toggle on or off: **Google Emergency Location Service**. This tells emergency services where you are if there's a problem. For example, if your car goes off the road and the ambulance needs to find you. You can turn this off if you want but read the fine print: "If ELS is off, your mobile carrier may still send device location during an emergency call." **Google Location Accuracy**. This uses Wi-Fi and other services to help pinpoint your location. If you want to turn off 'Use location' you need to make sure this is turned off as well. **Google Location History**. This leads you to a page where you can pause your device's collection of your location history. (That doesn't get rid of what's already been saved; this is covered in online privacy – see Chapter 6). **Google Location Sharing**. If you're sharing your location with family members or friends, you can manage it here.	

Disable your mobile ad ID

Your online activity can be tied together and tracked using your mobile advertising ID (also called IDFA and Android Advertising Identifier), which is a unique number created by your phone and sent to advertisers and app makers.

Since location data is sent along with your ad ID, it can be tied to other data about you. You can disable this feature entirely in your privacy settings, limiting the ways companies can tie your activities together.

> **On iOS**: Go to Settings > Privacy > Advertising and turn on Limit Ad Tracking.
>
> **On Android**: To find your Android Advertising Identifier, open the Google Settings app on your Android device and click on Ads. Your Advertising Identifier will be listed at the bottom of the screen.

Resetting an IDFA or Android Advertising Identifier may invalidate systems designed to respect your choices in advertising and may require you to submit any requests or forms again. If your advertising ID is shown as a string of only zeroes, your device is already set to limit ad tracking by default.

The ultimate method of stopping your phone being tracked is, of course, to turn it off. If you are likely to be in a very hostile environment, it's best to turn your phone off completely.

Phone lock screens

If your phone is lost or stolen it will probably be locked. You want to minimise what the thief can do from the lock screen, which has gone from having little useful information on it to become a billboard for notifications, alerts, and messages. Some of this information might be personal, and you might not want someone who is standing next to you to see it. If you leave your phone unattended on your desk, for example, anyone can see these notifications. By default, many features are available even if the screen is locked. For example, if you do lose the phone you will want to track it using Find My (iPhone) or Find My Device. You don't want the thief to be able to turn on airplane mode, which will prevent this. So, you should disable use of the Control centre from the lock screen, as described in Table 8.4 below.

Table 8.4 – How to disable the use of the control centre from the lock screen

Difficulty rating	
iOS	Navigate to Settings > Touch ID (or Face Id) & Passcode and disable Control Centre under 'Allow Access When Locked'. You may also want to disable notifications of messages. This will prevent thieves from seeing any two-factor codes that are sent to your phone via SMS.
	Go to Settings > Notifications > Show Previews and set it to either 'When Unlocked' or 'Never', as you prefer.
	You can also set the phone to erase all data after 10 failed attempts to enter the passcode.
	Go to Settings > Face ID & Passcode (or Touch ID) and enable Erase Data.
Android	There are myriad options concerning lock screens. Many Lock Screen apps have dubious security claims and almost as many ways to bypass the lock screen entirely. You should have a lock screen enabled though, as it's your first line of defence. Go to Settings > Security > Screen Lock. This will present a number of options:
	None: No lock screen security at all.
	Swipe: This option unlocks the device just by swiping on the lock screen. It's effectively the same as None.
	Pattern: Unlocks the device by using a specific swipe pattern along a series of nine dots. These can easily be copied if a thief sees you unlock the phone.
	PIN: Personal Identification Number. Choose at least six digits – ideally not your birthday!
	Password: This is the most cumbersome way to unlock your device but affords the most security if you choose a complex password.

Smart assistants

All phones offer virtual or 'smart' assistants these days. People seem to either love them or hate them, but from a security perspective they present more risks than benefits. Controlling your phone by voice while it is locked, such as allowing calls, could be a risk if the phone gets stolen. I would advise disabling smart assistants when the phone is locked but this is a matter of usability over security:

Difficulty rating	
iOS	Settings > Siri & Search and disable 'Allow Siri When Locked'. If you are coincerned that Apple is recording and storing your Siri interaction you can delete all recording by going to: Setting > Siri & Search > Siri & Dictation History and select 'Delete Siri & Dictation History' In any case I would advise that you opt out of sharing Siri data by going to: Settings > Analytics & Improvements and disabling 'Improve Siri & Dictation' (I actually disable them all).
Android	Google has not yet offered a simple solution. It's either always on or always off, but there is a workaround: 1. Launch the Google Assistant using the voice command or by holding down on the home button. Then tap on the box icon in the bottom left corner to open up the Assistant page. 2. Tap on your profile picture in the top right corner. In the following window, switch to the Assistant tab. 3. Select the Phone option from the Assistant devices list. 4. Disable the 'Access with Voice Match' option and then tap on OK in the pop-up that shows up next.

Free apps

Free apps are another area of concern. Many apps are free and perfectly trustworthy, and it's fair to say that the official app stores are relatively vigilant (far from perfect though) at rooting out the bad apples (no pun intended), so I'm not advocating a blanket voluntary ban. In any event, even the legitimate apps can present security problems[54] when used on an untrusted network, with 61% of Android applications and 36% of iOS applications sending users' data to remote servers.[55] Instead, I would urge you to check the app authors, independent third-party reviews, and feedback ratings before downloading any app – but most especially newly-added free ones as these represent the highest risk. Many free apps use advertising and tracking to generate revenue. Newer mobile operating systems such as iOS 14 force apps to prompt the user about tracking and require them to opt in. Always use a VPN when out and about on Wi-Fi, as mentioned earlier.

Bluetooth. Some Apps ask you to allow them to use Bluetooth. In many cases this is obvious, as they need to connect to a specific Bluetooth device, but some apps want to be able to search for Bluetooth location beacons in stores. This will effectively reveal your location and bypass the built-in location tracking. My advice would be to disallow Bluetooth connections unless it explains what the specific reason for allowing it is.

Every time you connect your phone to another device using Bluetooth you may be leaking data, so be careful. I recently hired a car and was just about to pair my phone with the vehicle's handsfree system when I noticed there was already a large number of contacts in the car system. Quickly scrolling down, I could see not only contact numbers but also notes stored as contacts, including PINs and passwords. I suspect the hire car company is supposed to wipe this data between

---

[54]   http://ieeexplore.ieee.org/document/7546508/?reload=true (unencrypted link)

[55]   Source Pradeo 2018 mobile threat landscape report www.pradeo.com

hires, but someone had forgotten on this occasion. My advice would be to either resist the temptation to upload contacts or, if you must, make sure you delete them when you are finished. Even though lots of people do it, you should not use your contacts app to store sensitive data such as PINs and passwords, as its not designed to hold that type of data.

While you have Bluetooth enabled, your phone can be identified by its name. If your phone is called "Sophie's iPhone" this could help an attacker approach you as if they know you. Better to call your phone something obscure or disable Bluetooth altogether. If you leave your device discoverable, you may be open to 'bluejacking'. This is an attack where unsolicited messages – usually inappropriate pictures – are sent to devices. It's often described as a harmless prank, but I've spoken to victims who found the experience unsettling to say the least. iPhones are always discoverable unless you disable Bluetooth.

Microphone and Camera. Users want to know if an app is using the microphone or camera on their phone or laptop. While newer versions of operating systems such as MacOS, Windows 10, and iOS 14 do offer indication that the camera or microphone are in use, my advice would be to take no chances – especially with laptops. Sliding camera covers are a few pennies and remove all the uncertainty.

AirDrop. A feature of iOS devices is AirDrop. It's a fast and convenient way to send items to nearby devices but there have been instances of people receiving unwanted images, sometimes called 'cyber flashing',[56] because they left AirDrop open to receive from anyone. To tighten these settings:

---

[56]   https://www.bbc.co.uk/news/uk-48054893

Difficulty rating	🌶️
iOS	Go to Settings > General > AirDrop and set it to Contacts Only or Receiving Off if you want to disable it. Note that AirDrop also uses Bluetooth, so if you disable Bluetooth you will also disable AirDrop.

Laptop security

If you travel often with a laptop then its security is probably a constant worry. Laptops are tempting targets for thieves, and the data on them is also of interest. Having a laptop stolen is annoying enough, but without good security measures you may lose a lot more than the device itself.

Lock screen

Firstly, you should ensure you have a lock screen enabled and a strong password (or biometric fingerprint or face id) to access the device.

Encryption — up to

Phones and tablets generally come with encryption enabled but laptops do not. This means that an unmodified laptop that is left on a bus could be opened and the hard disk copied, revealing all the data to the thief. Enabling encryption is fairly straightforward in most cases:

Difficulty rating	🌶️
MacOS	Apple MacBooks have a feature called 'FileVault' that can be enabled via System Preferences > Security & Privacy > FileVault. You will need to set a recovery key, which you must keep safe (write it down and put it in a drawer), as this is the only way to recover the data if you forget your password.
Windows 10	Windows laptops do not universally have this feature – called BitLocker – enabled by default, as it depends on your licence and whether or not your laptop has a feature called a Trusted Program Module or TPM. Press Windows+R to open a run dialog window. Type 'tpm msc' (no quotes) into it and press Enter to launch the tool. If you see information about the TPM in the PC – including a message at the bottom right corner of the window informing you which TPM specification version your chip supports – your PC does have a TPM so you can use bitlocker.

Difficulty rating	🌶️🌶️
Windows 10 (with a TPM)	To check if your windows laptop already uses BitLocker go to Control Panel > BitLocker Drive Encryption and you will see if it is enabled. If the option doesn't exist in Control Panel, then it is not supported so you might want to consider buying a third-party product to encrypt your data. If it is supported, then its easy to enable: 1. Click Start > Control Panel > System and Security (if the control panel items are listed by category), and then > BitLocker Drive Encryption. 2. Click Turn on BitLocker.

If your laptop doesn't have the required TPM but you have the right licence, it is still possible to use BitLocker although you will need to enter a password each time you start up the laptop/desktop. As

a general rule, the Professional and above licences do come with
BitLocker on newer laptops.

Difficulty rating	
Windows 10 without TPM	Before you do this, you should backup your laptop drive. You must use the Local Group Policy Editor to change the setting for your own PC. 1. To open the Local Group Policy Editor, press Windows+R on your keyboard, type "gpedit.msc" into the Run dialogue box, and press Enter. In the left-hand pane, navigate to Local Computer Policy > Computer Configuration > Administrative Templates > Windows Components > BitLocker Drive Encryption > Operating Sysem Drives. 2. You will see a list of policy settings on the right-hand pane. Double-click the 'Require additional authentication at start-up' option in the right pane. 3. Select 'Enabled; at the top of the window, and ensure the 'Allow BitLocker without a compatible TPM (requires a password or a start-up key on a USB flash drive)' checkbox is also enabled. 4. Click "OK" to save your changes. You can now close the Group Policy Editor window. 5. Finally, you can now turn on BitLocker in control panel. You'll first be asked how you want to unlock your drive when your PC boots up. If your PC had a TPM, you could have the computer automatically unlock the drive or use a short PIN that requires the TPM present. Because you don't have a TPM, you must choose to either enter a password each time your PC boots, or provide a USB flash drive. If you provide a USB flash drive here, you'll need that flash drive connected to your PC each time you boot up your PC to access the files. The BitLocker setup process creates a recovery key. It's essential that you photograph/record/save this key carefully because if you forget the password, this is the only way to access your drive once BitLocker is set. The BitLocker password only has to be entered when rebooting, so most of the time you will not notice it's there, but if your laptop gets lost or stolen you can be confident the data is safe, provided your everyday login password or PIN is strong, of course.

Securing the laptop against theft is one thing but if it gets stolen along with the bag, and the bag contains unencrypted USB disks or memory cards with all your precious data on, then its potentially disastrous. I would advise you to use modern encrypted USB drives which require a password or fingerprint to access. That way your data will be secure if it gets lost or stolen.

Chromebook security

Chromebooks are becoming very popular as the cheaper and simpler laptop alternative. They offer a very simple, sandboxed operating system, which anyone can learn their way around with minimal instruction, and since Android apps on Chromebooks are sandboxed from the core Chrome OS system, it's very hard to break that system.

Chromebooks sign in through a Google account so all the advice in earlier chapters around securing Google accounts applies to Chromebooks.

Chromebooks also use the Chrome browser so refer to the advice in Chapter 6 on cookies and browser privacy. The only 'gotcha' with Chromebooks is the lock screen setting, which is not always on.

To enable screen lock, select the clock at the bottom right. Select Settings. Click Screen lock and sign-in in the People section.

Enter your password and toggle on Show lock screen when waking from sleep.

If you have a long, complicated password that you'd rather not enter each time you wake up your Chromebook, select PIN or password and then click the Set up PIN button and choose a six-digit (or more) PIN that you can use instead of your password to unlock your Chromebook.

Wearables

A relatively new category of device is wearables – watches and fitness trackers being the most popular. Watches in particular are a risk as they can get left in lockers. Without a few security features, they present significant security risks.

Table 8.5 – Securing your smart watch

Difficulty rating	
Apple Watch	1. Enable Passcode Lock. Select Settings > Passcode, then choose Turn Passcode On and enter a code (again six digits is a lot better than four). To save having to enter it every time, enable Wrist Detection. 2. In the same section enable Erase Data, which will wipe the phone after 10 incorrect attempts. 3. Check Activation Lock is enabled by opening up the Watch app on your iPhone. Select the My Watch tab and then choose your watch's name on the screen. Hit the infomation icon and look for Find My Apple Watch. If you see that, the feature is active.
WearOS Watches	1. Wake up the watch. 2. From the top of the screen, swipe down. 3. Tap the Settings cog. 4. Scroll down and tap Personalisation, if present. 5. Tap Screen Lock. 6. Choose your pattern.

Our lives are increasingly mobile, and our devices often have direct access, via apps, to our online lives. Securing these devices is just as important as securing the online accounts they connect to.

Medicine is already making use of implanted devices that communicate to phones and other external sources. This trend is set to grow quickly over the next few years. So far their security track record has been far from perfect,[57] but we have no choice other than to place our security in the hands of the device manufacturers and the regulators. The good news is that standards[58] are emerging.

Video calling apps

Video calling has become very popular, largely as a result of the Covid-19 pandemic. During the early days, one of the more popular apps, Zoom, was the victim of a technique called 'Zoombombing' – a hacking technique that allowed eavesdropping on Zoom calls. This came about because people were careless in the way they used the app. All video meeting apps can potentially be 'bombed' if the meeting code is published widely. People were posting links to the meeting on social media, where their posting settings were public, and hackers were able to search for such posts and 'bomb' the meeting. It was a particular problem for schools and voluntary group meetings. There are several techniques to protect the meetings from such intrusion.

Firstly, the meeting id should be disseminated where possible using more private means, such as email or private messages. Secondly,

---

[57] https://www.researchgate.net/publication/327635202_Cybersecurity_Issues_in_Implanted_Medical_Devices

[58] Such as ISO 14971:2019

most video meeting apps have a 'lobby' or 'waiting room' feature that requires new arrivals to be admitted by the organiser. For smaller meetings this is a good way to control who can join. For larger meetings this may not be practical but use of a password (again carefully disseminated) can achieve the same result.

This book is aimed at personal rather than business security, so I have not covered other techniques such as muting all participants, preventing screen sharing, preventing recording etc. The National Cyber Security Centre offers guidance[59] for securing business video meetings.

---

[59] https://www.ncsc.gov.uk/guidance/
video-conferencing-services-security-guidance-organisations

Chapter 9: How to deal with an attack

If you have followed the preventative advice in this book, then you are much less likely to be a victim and therefore less likely to need to recover from an attack. However, it's fairly certain that at some point all of us will be victims of some sort of cyber attack or harassment. It may be that one of our online accounts is breached, or that we ourselves are targeted through our devices, or someone uses our digital footprint against us. In this chapter, I'm going to try and help you through the process.

One of the first questions people often ask when they discover an attack is: "Who has done this?" Who means you harm? It's not a nice thing to think about, is it? Most of us stumble through life generally believing we are liked by those around us, and any harm would be confined to a pickpocket, some mugger in an alley, or a teenager on a moped. In the cyber world we encourage companies to undergo something called threat modelling, which I'm going to adapt for use personally. Threat modelling looks at all of the groups (known in the parlance as 'Threat Actors') who may cause you harm – either deliberately or inadvertently – and categorises them. It then explores the motivations of each group, their capabilities and knowledge about the target, and the most likely way they would attack (or cause problems).

Let's adapt this process for our personal cyber life to build a general personal threat model. We need to think about who the threat actors are. Broadly they fall into four categories:

1. **Hacker groups**. These are not the hoodied characters often portrayed on TV. They are organised criminal gangs (OCGs) who are out for financial gain, so they're interested in things like extortion (via ransomware and other means), financial details (credit cards, bank accounts), access to shopping sites so they can buy goods using your money, and intercept/divert deliveries to their chain of 'mules' for cashing out. When we think of hackers, this is the group we tend to visualise. They are faceless and devoid of any conscience. What most people don't realise is the extent of the organisation behind these criminal enterprises.

   Hacker groups first came to the public attention during the Anonymous and Lulzsec attacks in 2011, but they have been around for much longer than that. Indeed, their origin dates back to the 1980s. I highly recommend Misha Glenny's book *Dark Market* if you want a detailed look into hacker groups and criminality. These groups are organised like businesses, with specific roles, and even employee benefits packages.

2. **Colleagues**. These are people you know at work or at school. They may be interested in you because they are jealous, or it may be that they have an unhealthy interest in you and your life. I would add schoolmates to this category for younger people. Sadly, bullying is now often about cyber stalking. According to the website comparitech.com,[60] 18% of UK schoolchildren were reported by parents as victims

---

[60] https://www.comparitech.com/internet-providers/cyberbullying-statistics/

of cyber bullying in 2018. The National Crime Agency puts the figure much higher at 43%. I'm not seeking to write a comprehensive guide to cyber bullying but rather focus on the practical steps you can take with your digital footprint to mitigate it. I provide links to cyber bullying resources at the end of the chapter.

3. **Friends and ex-partners**. Surely not! Well, I certainly hope not but it is a fact that stalking is on the rise with an increase of 28% in 2019.[61] The point here is they know a lot about you and that gives them a much higher capability level. They know most of your key dates, nicknames, pets' names, car registrations, music, and movie tastes – in other words your password 'themes' don't stand a chance. Cyber stalking is a crime in the UK (see panel below) but the essence of hacking is the sense that nobody will ever know it was you, and this tends to embolden attackers.

4. **Family**. This is less about malicious family-based attacks and more in the 'inadvertent' category. Many family members know each other's passwords, PINs (don't tell your bank), and regularly jump on each other's accounts to buy a pizza, rent a movie, take advantage of next day delivery, etc. The problem here is not your trusting them not to hack you; it's that you are relying on their operational security for your own resilience. Again, the Rock Solid password strategy (see Chapter 5) can be compromised by your child losing their phone, without a PIN, at school. That entry called 'mum's password' in the contacts list ...

---

[61] https://www.ons.gov.uk/peoplepopulationandcommunity/ crimeandjustice/datasets/crimeinenglandandwalesappendixtables

IT'S THE LAW: STALKERS

The Protection of Freedoms Act 2012 created two new offences of stalking by inserting new sections, 2A and 4A, into the Protection from Harassment Act 1997.

There's no strict legal definition of 'stalking', but section 2A (3) of the Protection from Harassment Act 1997 sets out examples of acts or omissions which, in particular circumstances, are ones associated with stalking, e.g. following a person, watching or spying on them, or forcing contact with the victim through any means, including social media.

I provide a list of stalking support resources at the end of the book.

The next step in a threat modelling process is to identify assets that might be attacked, but you've already done this in Chapter 3 when you mapped your footprint, and in Chapter 7 when you mapped your home network.

The final step is to consider what threats you are going to mitigate, and we have covered much of this in Chapters 4 to 8.

But what if your efforts fail, and you still get targeted? Let's focus on detection.

Attack Detection

Many people only find out they've been attacked once the damage has been done. So how can you tell if you've been a victim?

Breach notifications

If your data has been stolen as part of a data breach, you will likely hear about it from your account provider, i.e. the website that has been hacked. If it's a large data breach it may merit a story on the news. Around the time the TalkTalk attack was announced in 2015, criminals exploited TalkTalk customers by calling them using the stolen data to verify themselves, pretending to be calling with victim support, and attempting to defraud them by persuading them to download malware onto their computers.

If you hear about it on the news and you believe you are a victim, then don't wait for an official email from the company (this has been known to take days); act as soon as you reasonably can. If you're a customer in a data breach, you should go to the official website of the company (don't click links on any emails you receive about the attack) and follow the advice on that site. Sadly, not all companies are slick at this process and it may be a frustrating experience. In all cases it's a good idea to change your password for that account as soon as you reasonably can. Of course, if the compromised password is used elsewhere – especially with the same email address – you should change all those passwords as well, using (I hope) your password manager

But how will you know your account is compromised if a data breach has not been announced? Usually victims only find out when they notice an unusual transaction on a credit card or bank statement, so be sure to check these regularly. If you see an unusual transaction, report it to the card provider immediately. They will stop your card and you will not be liable for any fraud. Criminals often try a small transaction on a stolen card to test if it's active before they increase the amounts.

These are often for businesses in other countries, but increasingly they are for online purchases so should be fairly easy to spot. You will still not be sure which of your online accounts has been compromised at this stage, but you should raise your vigilance level and, for your most important accounts, consider changing your password. If the account supports two-factor authentication, you should turn this on.

My general advice would be to avoid saving your card details on websites wherever possible. Some sites like Amazon insist on have a card registered but for many you don't have to save the card details. In this way, if your account details are taken, the criminals won't have your card details, so you are less likely to become a fraud victim. Several password managers (covered in Chapter 5) can also store card details and fill them in for you on web pages, which is safer than trusting the website.

When you eventually discover which website your card details were stolen from, you should change any passwords for those accounts and enable two-factor authentication if it is supported. Of course, if you have reused the compromised password with other accounts – especially if the email is the same – you will also have to change all those passwords also. Take the opportunity to start using a password manager so that each account has a different strong password.

Let's assume you have used the same password across multiple sites, and it gets compromised. How could you tell if your online life was being watched by hackers? Or if your identity was being stolen? Here are some tips on how to help you detect when your personal accounts are being accessed.

Email and social media account tracking

All the large email providers and social media platforms allow you to view current and recent login activity. This is the best way to see if anyone else has logged into your accounts. The links for each major provider are shown in Table 9.1 below.

Table 9.1 – How to track your email and social media login activity

Difficulty rating 🌶️		
Provider	**Link for account activity**	**Spotting the stalkers**
Google	https://myaccount. google.com/ security?gar=1	You can remove any devices that look odd. Of course, that may mean the account is compromised. My advice would be to remove all devices and start over with 2FA enabled following a password reset.
Facebook	https://www. facebook.com/ settings?tab=security	You can click 'end all activity' to force all devices to log out. Of course, you should change passwords and enable 2FA on a trusted device before logging in anywhere else.

Hotmail/ Live.com	https://account.live. com/Activity	You can see all recent login activity. Helpfully Microsoft also shows a map of where it believes the login was located. If you select a login event you are concerned about you can secure your account from the link provided, which will start the password reset process.
Twitter	https://twitter.com/ settings/applications	You can log out of all other sessions if you see anything that doesn't look right. You should change passwords and enable 2FA on a trusted device before logging in anywhere else.
LinkedIn	https://www.linkedin. com/psettings/sessions	You can sign out of all sessions or individually You should change passwords and enable 2FA on a trusted device before logging in anywhere else.
Yahoo	https://login.yahoo. com/account/ activity?src=noSrc	You can remove any devices that look odd. That may mean the account is compromised so you may need to change passwords. My advice would be to remove all devices and start over with 2FA enabled following a password reset.

There are apps which can take the legwork out of this process for you. Also, many of the main providers now alert you each time there is a login from a new location or device. Don't ignore these alerts as they may indicate your account has been compromised. Blocking the access isn't enough; you will also need to log in and change your password, and switch on two-factor authentication to protect the account. If you have inadvertently allowed access but then realise it was dodgy, you should immediately log in and report the issue so that your account can be protected. This is where your backup email account becomes essential, and why it needs the same level of protection.

Email rules

Some more sophisticated hackers and stalkers, once they gain access to your email, will create 'rules' (effectively filters) in your account to prevent you from seeing any 'password reset' emails or warnings from your providers about their activity. They may also try to change your 'recovery' email address to allow themselves a way back in should you change your password. You can check this by visiting your account settings/preferences and if you see any rules you didn't add yourself, then you have definitely been compromised. Delete the rules, check your backup email/mobile number is correct, and then change your password to lock them out. In case they have a current login still live, make sure all activity is ended using the above links in Table 9.1. You should then check that your backup email is also secure. Do make sure that your backup email actually exists, or you just made the stalker's life easy as they can simply create that account and get a back door without doing any work. Links to access your email rules and how to set up a recovery email address are in Table 9.2 below.

Table 9.2 - How to access your email rules

Difficulty rating		
Provider	**Link for email rules**	**Recovery email link**
Hotmail / Live.com	https://outlook.live.com/mail/0/options/mail/rules	https://account.live.com/proofs/manage/basic
Google Mail (Gmail)	https://mail.google.com/mail/u/0/?tab=wm#settings/filters	https://myaccount.google.com/security?gar=1
Yahoo	https://mail.yahoo.com/d/settings/7	https://login.yahoo.com/account/security

It's fair to say that if you have added two-factor authentication, then once you have checked there are no rules, you should be OK going forward.

Response

Let's postulate that none of this has worked and they have still got in, and you only find out once something bad has happened. As well as regaining access to your accounts, you need to protect your identity. I've provided an account recovery checklist below. If the compromised account is important (such as email), then whether or not you succeed in recovering the account(s) at this stage, you should call in professional help from an identity protection specialist, and report the matter (in the UK) to Action Fraud and CIFAS and, of course, your bank and your lenders.

For an administration fee, CIFAS – the UK's fraud prevention service – can place a 'Protective Registration' warning on your credit file. This will tell lenders that you think your personal information is at risk of being used fraudulently. When a lender receives an application with your details, they'll make extra checks to make sure the person applying is you and not a fraudster. The main credit reference agencies, Equifax and Experian, offer guidance in this scenario. This will probably mean that you get called whenever you seek to open a new account, but at least you'll get peace of mind.

In any event you should sign up for a credit reporting and alerting service so that any new cards or loans are alerted to you. This is a good idea, anyway, as keeping an eye on your credit report is a useful way of finding out that something may not be right.

Account recovery checklist

If you find you're locked out of an account and/or suspect it's been hacked, here is a checklist for recovering the account.

1. Make sure your devices are up to date. Before you begin, make sure that the Operating Systems and apps on the devices you use are up to date. These updates will install the latest security fixes.
2. If it's a laptop or desktop, run a full antivirus scan.
3. If you think your router may have been hacked, the first step is to try to connect to it. If you bought the router, check the manual for the web address to enter into your browser and the default login and password information. If your Internet provider supplied the router, contact their support department to find out what to do.

   If you're not able to login, then consider resetting your router – though be sure to check with your Internet provider to find out any settings you'll need to configure to reconnect after you reset it. When your reset router restarts, connect to it, and set a strong administrative password

4. If it's a website account and you can't access it, go to the account provider homepage, and find a link to their help or support pages. These will detail the account recovery process.
5. If your email account was hacked, then there are some things you should check once you get back in. Check for any email filters and forwarding rules (see Table 9.2 above).

6. Change passwords – you will likely have set a new password to regain control, but if the old password was shared, then change it everywhere to a unique password for each account. Now would be a good time to get a password manager and enable 2FA.

7. Lastly, with email and social media accounts you should notify your contacts. It's embarrassing but they should be warned in case the hackers contacted them through your hacked account.

8. If you can't recover your account, then document everything; take screenshots, etc and send the evidence to the service provider, and keep a copy. It may be that you need to create a new account if the old account has been used for criminal activity. Once the new account is in place, you will need to contact everyone who used the old one (if it was email). This alone is an incentive to put the security in place to prevent the attack. The thought of losing my email account(s) is too awful to contemplate.

9. Contact Action Fraud.[62]

Blocking and reporting abuse

For many people targeted by stalkers, bullies, or trolls the temptation to block them is strong. While blocking goes a long way to preventing the emotional harm of cyberbullying, there are still a few ways that stalkers and bullies can work around it. A few examples:

---

[62] https://www.actionfraud.police.uk/

- Someone who stalks your profile on Instagram or Facebook can still follow your friends' accounts, and see photos that you're tagged in.
- If the stalker or cyberbully shares your private information or photos, they can keep doing this even if you block them on one platform.
- Cyberbullies can just create new accounts. Most sites only require a username and email address to sign up, so there isn't a huge barrier to entry.

Blocking should always be done alongside reporting the abuse to the platform provider where possible. All the main social media platforms have a reporting mechanism. I list the main ones below.

Table 9.3 – Reporting Abuse

Difficulty rating	🌶
Provider	**Abuse Reporting**
Facebook	Facebook offers a way to report any comments on your timeline. https://www.facebook.com/help/1753719584844061?helpref=hc_global_nav
Instagram	Instagram offers a way to report any posts on your timeline. https://help.instagram.com/192435014247952
Twitter	Twitter offers a block and a report feature for each tweet and reply. https://help.twitter.com/en/safety-and-security/report-abusive-behavior

Ransomware Attacks

So far, we have focussed on the type of hacking that infiltrates your accounts with the purpose of stealing your information, identity, or access to funds. A common current type of attack is ransomware-extortion. This doesn't need the attacker to break into your account. They just need you to click on a link or (more usually) download and run some malware. This then proceeds to encrypt all your documents, pictures, videos, and other files - on all the drives it can access[63] – and then demands that you pay a ransom (in bitcoin) to retrieve the data. If such an attack gets past you and your internet security software what can you do? it is sometimes possible for infected users to regain access to their encrypted files or locked systems, without having to pay. The website

https://www.nomoreransom.org/

is a community project to make ransomware recovery tools available. Users upload an encrypted file and the site will tell you if it can recover the original. In many cases it will not be able to but it's worth a try.

Beware of searching for ransomware recovery tools. Often as not these are malware themselves. If they are provided by a commercial security software company or nomoreransom.org then they are trustworthy and may work but don't rely on hope. Hope is not a strategy.

---

[63] This may include your Windows File History drive if you have this feature enabled. https://support.microsoft.com/en-gb/help/4013550/windows-protect-your-pc-from-ransomware

You now only really have two choices.

Firstly, you can pay. Ransom amounts vary from a few hundred pounds to several thousand (and more). If you can afford to pay and you feel you have no choice, then will you get your files back? Generally, yes you will but it's far from guaranteed, these are criminals after all. When the ransom is paid you will typically be provided with some software to decrypt most (but sometimes not all) of your encrypted files. If you have no backups, then your hands are tied but I would generally advise against paying if the alternative is open to you. Paying the ransom encourages more ransomware, and in many cases the unlocking of the encrypted files is not successful. Payment is almost always via Bitcoin so you will need to buy some from a reputable trading site. Coinbase.com is often cited as the easiest for newcomers.

The second choice is to restore your files from good recent backups. Having a good backup regime has never been more important. For many of us we rely on the fact that files are 'in the cloud' but it's worth investing in some good cloud backup services that take fresh copies of changed files on a daily basis. I am a little obsessive and have a home Network Access Storage system (NAS) and cloud backups as well as some long-term archives of pictures. Many people rely on keeping everything on their phones but even with larger memories and cloud storage these can get deleted either by accident or maliciously. In a ransomware scenario your backups can be the only thing protecting your digital memories.

The surest way of being certain that malware or ransomware has been removed from a system is to do a complete wipe of all storage devices and reinstall everything from scratch. Formatting the hard disks in your system will ensure that no remnants of the malware remain. Most laptops offer a 'restore to factory settings' option. This will generally be enough to remove the ransomware and get your laptop ready to copy your backed-up files onto it. Select a backup or backups that was made prior to the date of the initial ransomware infection to avoid re-infecting your recovered system.

Common scams and extortion attempts

I'm going to end this chapter with a description of a few well-known scams to make you aware of the most common ones. These change fast (at the time of writing there are a spate of scams around the coronavirus, for example).

Many scams share similar features or signs that can make them easier to identify. Scammers seek to gain your trust by claiming to be a business you have heard of or even someone you know; they will offer ways to 'verify' their trustworthiness by sending you to a website; they will offer something that has a time limit or a scarcity to get you to make decisions without thinking; lastly they will often appeal to your emotions. Of course, these are not unique to scams, but most scams have several of these elements. It's also wrong to think that smart people don't fall for scams – research from the University of Exeter showed that on the contrary, scam victims put more cognitive effort in analysing scams than non-victims.

Porn password emails – these consist of an email telling you that they have your password and they have evidence of you watching pornography. They can sometimes include all or part of your password as a 'convincer'. These scammers have recovered a password associated with your email from a data breach and are relying on you reusing that password everywhere to trick/shame you into parting with 'hush' money. They have no such evidence, but if the password they have provided is current, you should swiftly move to reset all accounts where that password is used. If it's an old password, then you have nothing to worry about. Either way, don't respond to the email or part with any money.

'Change your IP address' – these scams consist of a call and sometimes an accompanying email telling you that your computer has been compromised by malware or hackers, and that you need to change your 'IP address'. The caller will claim to be from Microsoft or your phone provider. None of this is true. Your IP address is provided by your Internet Service Provider and has nothing to do with your security. The scammers are trying to get you hooked into a call whereby you will download some software and give control of your computer to them while they 'fix' the problem. At best they are trying to get you to buy an expensive support arrangement through false pretences, and at worst they will hack all your accounts and steal your data. Just put the phone down and block the caller. UK Finance have current advice on widely used scams at https://takefive-stopfraud.org.uk/

If you fall for a scam and realise later that you have done so, then try to gather some evidence – screenshots, etc. and put them in a safe place before you start the process of resetting everything. If you believe your computer/phone/tablet has been infected, then the only sure-fire solution is to back everything up and go through a full factory reset process. For mobile phones and tablets, visit the manufacturer's support website.

In the case of a computer, this can be a time-consuming process. Don't just rely on your antivirus to detect malware as the hackers may have used customised malware that will not be detected. Instead, rebuild from scratch – most modern laptops/desktops with Windows 10 have a recovery option that allows a full factory reset. You can usually access this by pressing F8 during the boot process. From there, it's manufacturer-specific so visit their website for vendor advice. For Apple Macs, the advice can be found at https://support. apple.com/en-gb/HT201065.

Chapter 10: What does the future hold?

Will we be more or less secure as we get older? Will devices become 'secure by design'? Will companies and websites find ways to stop being hacked? Will we be able to protect our data such that it can sit in the cloud and be totally secure?

Much of what I have been commenting on in this book has come about as a result of the extreme pace of technological change not being tracked by an equivalent pace of security change. Add to this the tendency for users – both companies and individuals – to cling to outdated security practices, and you get a security gap into which the hackers move and exploit. Is this gap closing? Yes, I think so, but not as fast as I would like to see. The public mood (especially the regulators' mood) has shifted, and most providers now have to put security somewhere near the top of their agenda. Once security becomes a significant part of the consumer's buying decision, we are winning. This will take a few years to become the norm, but I do see real change. The problem is that many businesses are still relying on legacy systems and can't afford to just swap them out for the latest. But even here I see real progress towards a more secure future. There will be an impact on us as users. We will have to adopt new security behaviours. For example, multi-factor (or two-step) authentication will become the norm, and this will make a real difference. The cost to the attackers will rise significantly, and so many will leave the field of play. Twenty years ago, car stereo theft was a real problem but very few get stolen today, largely because the stereos became integrated into the car, making them much harder to steal. The solution was to design the problem out of the system. Internet security has to go the same way. If credential theft is an issue, then we need new ways of accessing systems that don't need a username and a password. This is beginning to happen with federated identity management services, such as 'sign in with Apple' and the like, which use your phone as a trusted token to authorise your login. Of course, there is the 'eggs in baskets' fear, but I see these services becoming increasingly popular because they are easy to use and require no passwords – just your phone biometric. The ubiquity of biometrics on phones and tablets, both face and fingerprint, and the rapid advent of similar features on laptops, means that within five years these devices will no longer present a viable target for the vast majority of attackers. There are already providers using 'authenticator apps', such as Google and Microsoft, which simply require you to authorise any login using the app on your phone. The passwords are still there but you just can't see them anymore. In this way, passwords will become largely a thing of the past for users. They will still exist for years in the background, but we won't be aware of them because our phones will seamlessly log in for us.

With voice rapidly replacing other forms of interaction with computers it is only a matter of time before keyboards and mice are replaced and traditional computing environments become intuitive experiences where we are removed from the underlying operating system and our voice biometric will be recognised as our 'user name'.

This will inevitably mean that the hackers will increasingly seek to get malware onto phones and digital assistants. Dubious apps and free games will become the vehicle to attempt to take control of devices and subvert these secure login processes. The good news is that modern devices come with much better security architectures, making this type of attack much harder – not impossible (never impossible) – but much harder.

Several banks are already using zero login or password-less login for their mobile apps. Instead of a password they send you an email link. This worries me, as email remains a legacy technology that providers should not be relying on and, as I've already covered, email is a weak spot that attackers often target.

All these technologies have the benefit of being more secure and easy to use, so will inevitably gain traction. For the average user, the problems will be in the margins. Those providers that still don't require 2FA or use the phone as a secure login device will still use the good old password, and we will be right back where we started.

It is my hope that in future as users we will not "see the joins" of security as it will be fully integrated into the service we are using. To use a car analogy, this means we will be able to simply drive a vehicle instead of having to be a home mechanic.

All of the above still relies on a security model where the service providers keep your data, but what if there was a way in which *you* kept all your data? Sir Tim Berners Lee, the inventor of the World Wide Web, has postulated just such an idea. The SOLID security architecture is based on the notion that users keep all their data in digital vaults called PODs. App providers and websites can be granted temporary access to the data but can't copy it or keep it; they can just use it for a specific transaction. The security, of course, rests on the PODs, but this is a good thing. By having all the data in a few places, security can be designed into the system. The SOLID concept is still new, but it does exist and is getting a lot of attention. For many website and app owners, it sounds like adoption would be like turkeys voting for Christmas, as they lose access to those huge datasets which they can monetise, but there's no reason they couldn't have access to each of our PODs by agreement, or for a small fee. It would radically change the financial model underpinning the Internet, but it would largely design out security issues, and hacking would be much less attractive or profitable.

So, does this mean everything will be secure? Not by a long chalk! Even if concepts such as SOLID become the norm, there will still be new ways the hackers can break in, although the attacker cost will be very high indeed, so I would expect the volume of attacks to fall dramatically.

However, there's one very large category that I haven't covered in terms of future gazing: the Internet of Things.

The Internet of Things (IoT)

From a security perspective, this is a complete mess. The almost total absence of standards or regulations means that the 'cheapest tech wins' in almost every case, and this inevitably means little or no security. Will this change in future?

I suspect that it won't change for some time. The marketplace is very young and chaotic, and there are few incentives for manufacturers to invest in security just now. The privacy legalisation regimes in Europe and elsewhere will certainly help, but it will be a long time before all devices come with a 'secure by design' sticker or similar. When you consider the enormous variety and volume of data that IoT devices collect (now and in the future), it makes all the effort to secure our social media accounts seem a bit pointless. In overall terms we will be less secure as we adopt more IoT. Perhaps we have been fighting the battles in the wrong place. There is room for some optimism though. Legislation requiring that IoT devices on sale meet certain minimum standards, as we do today with products such as toys, could be just around the corner. The Information Commissioner in the UK already has an Age Appropriate Design Code and the UK government is consulting on a wider IoT code of practice. These standards will be in areas such as preventing default passwords, requiring the ability to self-update, and the use of encrypted communications. This would place a burden on manufacturers and retailers, and might be difficult to implement (especially online), but it could move the dial such that most of us would buy devices that have some security built in.

Artificial intelligence (AI)

What about artificial intelligence (AI)? AI is being used increasingly by companies as part of their security. At the moment it is mostly being used to monitor network activity to detect hackers and fraudsters, but it is finding uses in many security contexts, such as face recognition, and this is causing public concern. Use of face tracking in retail settings or on the high street has caused controversy. Some companies have distanced themselves from face recognition technology, and some have asked for regulation of its use.

For many of us, our first obvious encounter with AI has been through digital assistants such as Amazon Echo or Google Home, and there's considerable suspicion about the privacy and security implications of such devices. These assistants are increasingly taking the burden of our busy lives: reminding us when we need to go shopping, turning lights and heating on and off, and playing us rain forest noises to help us sleep. Use of AI is rapidly expanding in the home security arena. Integrating cameras, microphones, and lights may make our homes more secure.

My advice would be to carefully read privacy notices where AI is involved and take a cautious approach. Try to determine how images, recordings, and histories are stored, and delete according to your risk appetite. In the UK there is no specific legal provision for the regulation of the development of AI or the use of AI applications. The most obvious protection could come via the Data Protection Act regulated by the Information Commissioner's Office, but the question is whether the ICO will have the institutional capacity and expertise to use its powers in respect of AI, or will sufficiently prioritise doing so against the competing demands on its limited resources. This is important because I believe the area where AI could have the biggest impact on our personal lives and privacy is in healthcare, not self-driving cars. All of the major AI providers are working with healthcare data, and privacy issues have been reported. Within 10 years I believe initial medical or mental health consultation with be through your smart home assistant, followed up by a video consultation, again via your smart assistant device or phone. The practitioner may not even be fully qualified but may rely on an AI diagnostic assistant. All of this will require your most personal data to be shared without any anonymity. The regulatory regime (as usual) has some catching up to do.

New types of attack will develop using the latest technology. Phishing emails will be generated by AI and will become even harder to spot. Deepfake technology will mean that many forms of media will become untrustworthy as hackers doctor images, audio, and video to help perpetuate their crimes.

What will be our expectation of privacy in the future? There are many who feel that any expectation of privacy is an outdated concept but I don't subscribe to this view. Digital natives such as millennials are better at compartmentalising their lives such that they keep the data they want to protect separate from the data they are happy to share.

This is one area where service providers can help. If there are clear indications whenever data is added to the platform as to who will be able to see it, it will be much easier for us to control our privacy.

As things stand the pace of change (or progress, if you prefer) is increasing, but even though security and privacy are now sometimes on their agenda, they are at best playing catch-up, so we as users must act as the regulator by scrutinising the security of each system or device we purchase or interact with compared to our risk appetite. This is becoming unsustainable, and we are all tacitly accepting ever greater security and privacy risks as each day passes. It's important to get a grip on our digital footprints as they stand, reduce them where we can, and change our buying behaviours to scrutinise what each new service or product is going to do to that footprint going forwards.

Wherever you stand on privacy and security – relaxed or risk-averse – it's now part of the new normal to have to question the security that comes with a product or service, and to understand the privacy implications of using it. There are no silver bullets on the horizon, but it's not necessary to be an expert to be able to keep your risks tolerable and still enjoy the benefits of our amazing connected world.

I do think, however, that before we reach this Nirvana, we will suffer some major attacks that will affect many millions or even billions of individuals. Unfortunately, history shows us that it is only these wake-up calls that make significant change possible. I fervently hope that the platform providers don't need this level of event to persuade them, but my experience tells me otherwise.

If you follow the advice in this book your data has a better chance of surviving such an event and, furthermore, if you follow my advice you are less likely to be a victim in the first place and more likely to be able to live your digital life in relative ease.

References and sources

Cyber stalking: An Analysis of Online Harassment and Intimidation –
Michael L Pittaro, 2007[64]

Support services, help and advice

Stalking Help and Advice

https://www.suzylamplugh.org/stalking-help-and-advice

Safety

https://www.getsafeonline.org/

Cyber Bullying

https://www.nationalbullyinghelpline.co.uk/contact.html

---

[64] https://www.cybercrimejournal.com/pittaroijccvol1is2.htm

About the author

Paul Vlissidis is one of the founders of NCC Group's Technical Security Consulting division and started NCC Group's penetration testing (ethical hacking) team in 1997. He was one of the founders of the international industry body representing the technical security industry, CREST, for which he is now a Fellow. He held the role of Chief Information Security Officer at NCC for five years and now advises senior business leaders on all aspects of cyber security and resilience. Having led the cyber team on the popular Channel 4 show *Hunted*, Paul has (ethically) hacked hundreds of people over the six seasons of the show. He is an authority on personal cyber resilience and has several publications on the subject.

Paul is father to three grown-up children.

Printed in Great Britain
by Amazon

30007076R00126